HOW TO GROW FOOD
FOR YOUR FAMILY

How to Grow FOOD For Your Family

BY

SAMUEL R. OGDEN

Drawings by
W. W. FAULKS

Completely Revised and Edited

1974

LITTLEFIELD, ADAMS & CO.
Totowa, New Jersey

Published 1974 by
LITTLEFIELD, ADAMS & CO.

by arrangement with A. S. Barnes & Co.

©A. S. Barnes, 1973

Library of Congress Cataloging in Publication Data

Ogden, Samuel R.
  How to Grow Food for Your Family

  (A Littlefield, Adams Quality Paperback No. 280)
  Reprint of the ed. published by A. S. Barnes,
  South Brunswick.
  1. Vegetable gardening.   I. Title.
[SB321.034   1974]   635   74-2398
ISBN 0-8226-0280-6

Printed in the United States of America

CONTENTS

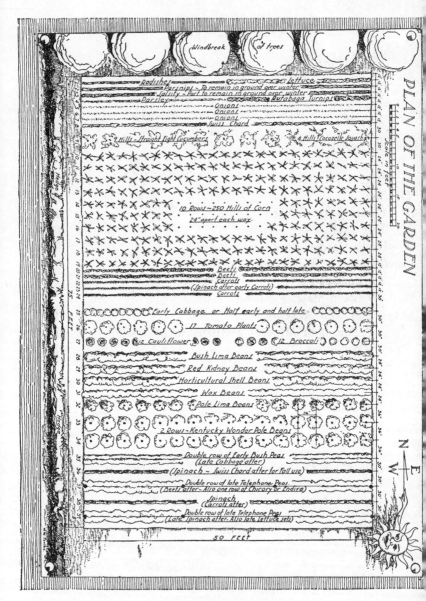

PLAN OF THE GARDEN

Windbreak of trees

Radishes
Parsnips ~ To remain in ground over winter
Salsify ~ Part to remain in ground over winter
Parsley
Rutabaga Turnips
Onions
Onions
Onions
Swiss Chard

9 Hills ~ Straight Eight Cucumbers   4 Hills Cocozelle Squash

10 Rows ~ 250 Hills of Corn
24" apart each way.

Beets
Beets
Carrots
(Spinach after early Carrots)
Carrots

Early Cabbage   or Half early and half late

17   Tomato Plants

12 Cauliflower   12 Broccoli

Bush Lima Beans

Red Kidney Beans

Horticultural Shell Beans

Wax Beans

Pole Lima Beans

2 Rows ~ Kentucky Wonder Pole Beans

Double row of Early Bush Peas
(Late Cabbage after)
(Spinach ~ Swiss Chard after for Fall use)

Double row of late Telephone Peas.
(Beets after ~ Also one row of Chicory or Endive)

Spinach
(Carrots after)

Double row of late Telephone Peas
(Late Spinach after ~ Also late Lettuce sets)

50 FEET

Lettuce

N
E
W

Plan of the Garden

FOREWORD

MY FATHER was raised in the country and when circumstances brought him to the city, where I was born, his love of the soil came with him. Fortunately, our city home had a big yard; and a good bit of that yard was devoted to a vegetable garden which was at once my father's hobby and his delight.

Almost as soon as I was old enough to distinguish a weed from a vegetable I was impressed into service. I could not understand my father's enthusiasm for such drab pleasures, and eagerly looked forward to the time when I might be my own master and escape the drudgery of gardens. It did not seem possible to me then that some day I would really enjoy digging in the earth, that I would experience keen pleasure in planting and thinning and weeding.

So let no one with memories of childhood hours spent in thinning carrots while the crash of ball against bat could be heard in the lot over the fence, be convinced that even now he would not like gardening. Manifold pleasures, I can assure him, and above all a satisfying sense of accomplishment, await the man who grows a successful garden.

There are even esthetic rewards. A well-kept vigorous vegetable garden, its rows trim and straight, devoid of weeds, only the alternate rows of chocolate earth and green vegetation of varying shades and textures, is a thing of real beauty. To me it is more beautiful than a flower garden. When I was working among the vegetables one evening, a six-year-old came out to watch me. He stood a moment, hands on hips, looking at the garden. Then he exclaimed enthusiastically, "It's—beautiful!"

Because circumstances and environment vary so greatly, it is impossible to give hard-and-fast rules for garden procedure. No statement can be made that will fit all conditions of soil and climate. Generalizations and suggestions are useful, however; and the experience gained in one garden can be modified and adapted as a guide for any other garden. Nothing is as helpful as first-hand experience, of course. Fortunately, it is easy to acquire, and the cost of mistakes is negligible.

It is the aim of this handbook to stimulate interest in subsistence gardening and to help the beginner with some of the fundamental problems. It is based on many years of sound experience in growing vegetables.

It is my sincere hope that those who have suitable land available for gardening will put it to use; and that those who now have some sort of garden will increase its size, if possible, and give it the care and attention necessary to produce a satisfying harvest. I trust that this book may be of assistance to them; that an increasingly large number of people may experience the joy and the many benefits to be derived from growing their own vegetables.

S. R. O.

This new edition has been updated to include improved varieties of vegetables and methods of, insect and disease control developed since the book was first published. Because new developments take place constantly it is suggested that the vegetable grower obtain the latest information prior to each growing season from the U.S. Department of Agriculture or the local state agricultural representative.

CHAPTER I

WHY A GARDEN?

IN THE TIME of our grandfathers and great-grandfathers far more people, proportionately, lived in the country. And in each family, from half-grown children up to grandparents, everyone was busy from sunrise to sunset. They were busy living. They had to be sheltered from the weather, be clothed, fed, and to have some surplus of material goods laid up against the future.

They felled their trees and cut the timbers to frame the house or barn, hewing them into shape; they split the shingles from spruce or hemlock blocks. They raised sheep and clipped, cleaned and carded the wool; they spun the wool into yarn and wove the yarn into the cloth of which they made their clothes. They grew flax and made their own linens. They made their soap with fat and wood ashes. They tapped the sugar maples in spring and made their sugar. They battled with the soil, the rain and wind and frosts to raise wheat, which was ground into flour; from the flour they made their own bread. They raised flocks and herds that they might have wool and hides and meat. They made their own butter and cheese.

The land produced the things whereby they lived; there was a direct relationship between human life and the soil. Even in the cities this was no doubt apparent and real. In these days of great concentration of populations, of specialization and industrialization, this fundamental relationship has almost completely been lost. Yet it is an integral part of the race heritage of each one of us. To lose our contact with the soil results in real un-ease and maladjustment; to recapture it affords profound joy and inward comfort.

Besides, there are tangible results, the production of usable things. The produce of even a modest plot of land, properly treated, will substantially and favorably affect the family budget. Records of the United States Department of Agriculture show that under favorable conditions the time spent in the garden yields a return equal to that obtained for a corresponding period devoted to regular employment. It has been estimated that a vegetable garden can be made to reduce the amount of money spent for food to the extent of 5 to 10 per cent of the average salary.

In Vermont, and many other States, there is a slack time in the farmer's year toward the end of March and the beginning of April. Snow is still in the woods and frost is in the ground. The sun is hot and sap begins to run, but the frost and the snow and the mud will not permit the soil to be worked. So it is at this time that the farmer taps his sugar maples, and turns to the making of maple sugar and syrup. By dint of hard work —often, when the sap is running freely, he is at the sugarhouse boiling all night long—he turns out a product that has real cash value.

It requires about thirty gallons of sap to make one gallon of syrup. Under favorable conditions one tree will yield seven or eight gallons of sap, or about one quart of syrup. The financial rewards in terms of labor are not great. But, and here is the point, the time spent on this very pleasant occupation would be otherwise more or less wasted, and the money is received at a time when it is most welcome.

The case of the home gardener might be considered a parallel one. Time wasted, or used on non-profitable hobbies, can well be spent in the garden, adding a substantial sum to the family income and at the same time fulfilling, in a most healthful and satisfying manner, the need that all of us have for a hobby.

One of the many advantages in having your own garden, in growing your own vegetables, is the privilege of choosing the varieties that you prefer. The vegetables on sale at the green-grocer's are produced commercially and of necessity are varieties that were not selected for their flavor or succulence, but for their ability to stand the rough treatment of machine methods of cultivation and harvesting, as well as for their hardiness to endure long shipments and many handlings. The home gardener, on the other hand, has a wide choice, alluringly displayed in the seed catalogues. He can choose on a purely personal basis, his selection governed only by the requirements of the family and the exigencies of the climate in which he lives. Thus he can place all the emphasis on texture and flavor.

Anyone who has delved into a seed catalogue knows its fascination. And as the home gardener may select any variety he chooses—of the many that will thrive in his climate—the attractive descriptions and the tempting photographs are likely to inspire him to great flights of self-expression.

Turn, for instance, to the page of cabbages, and experience the seduction of the seed catalogue. Shall you be conservative and stick to the Danish type your neighbor grows? "A solid round-head variety of excellent quality. The plant is compact with few outer leaves and a short stem. A market and kraut cabbage." Or, shall you go fancy and try "Savoy: The plants are medium large, producing deep, rounded heads, and moderately solid. The variety is admired for its crumpled, dark bluish-green leaves and creamy white interior. The flavor and quality are distinctive and it stores well." Or shall you try Chinese cabbage? "Chihli: A tall sure-headed variety. The outer dark-green leaves enclose a long, tapering head. The head is very compact, white tinted with green, crisp and sweet. This is sometimes called celery cabbage."

If it is cucumbers that interest you, you may be allured by the "Chicago Pickling: The most widely used variety, particularly adapted for large pickles. The fruits are thick; uniform, medium-green, and square-ended. The plants are very prolific." Or possibly you may choose the "Straight Eight: An early variety producing cylindrical symmetrical smooth fruits, well rounded at the ends. When ready for use the color is deep green and the fruit is free from light tips and stripes. Highly productive." Very likely you will end by ordering both!

There is a thrilling decision to make at every turn of the page, in the whole fascinating catalogue. And this preliminary choosing, listing and ordering the varieties that *you* want to grow, is but a small part of the pleasure that you will derive from having a vegetable garden of your own.

A decidedly important reason for the home garden is that the vegetables can be gathered for immediate table use, and when they have reached precisely the proper stage of maturity to be at their best. For instance, sweet corn should be cooked and on the table within a half-hour of being picked, or certainly not more than an hour or two. Its sugar content dissipates rapidly after the corn is removed from the stalk; the longer it has been picked the more tasteless and tough it is.

Vegetables from your own garden, used soon after picking, not only have a higher vitamin content, but in other ways are superior to those grown commercially, some of which have been picked slightly green to facilitate handling and shipping. Nothing can compare with a vine-ripened tomato plucked right off the plant and eaten still warm from the sun. Celery and salads, crisp with morning dew, cannot be compared with those which have been wilted, watered, and chilled before coming to the table. Peas, picked fresh from the garden, shelled and popped right into the pot and soon served, are an entirely different vegetable from the peas bought at the store. The difference between home-grown vegetables and those on the market is truly great, and one that once experienced will set new standards of excellence, and will establish the taste value of vegetables.

The primary consideration, in planning a garden, is of course the land. If you have a choice of sites, the location of the garden must be considered. If possible, it should be on a slightly sloping piece of ground, and one that faces to the southeast. This is the ideal exposure, as it not only gets more hours of sunlight, but is partially protected from the north and northwest winds. Whatever the location, however, it is wise to have the garden site protected by shrubbery or buildings from the cold winds from the north and northwest.

The garden should be free from shade, and should not be near trees, which not only will deprive it of sunlight but will rob it of plant foods and moisture.

If you live in the country where there is plenty of room and wild life as well, it will be wise to have it very near the house, so that it may come under your frequent surveillance. Vegetable gardens planted away from the house are certain to be marauded by whatever herbivorous animals there are in the neighborhood; it does not take them long to discover where they can get a delectable meal.

Having chosen the location, the size of the plot is determined by three important factors: the amount of usable land available; the size of the family the garden is to serve; and the amount of time that can be devoted to garden work.

If a small plot only is available, there must be consideration of the kinds of vegetables to be planted, and of those which can be dispensed with. Potatoes will be eliminated, for they require a great deal of space; so, too, do melons, squashes and pumpkins. Perhaps no one in the family likes parsnips; if so no parsnips need be planted. Staple winter vegetables, such as turnips and cabbages, which can be purchased reasonably at any store, may be eliminated. Others may be omitted, such as a few long-season vegetables which would occupy the ground during the entire season.

In starting a garden with no fund of experience to draw upon, one might be bewildered by the seeming problem of size. But it is no problem. If you have a space in your back yard twenty by thirty feet, that is sufficient for a garden. If you are fortunate enough to have unlimited space, there is still no problem. You need only bear in mind the size of your family and the amount of time that you or others can devote to work in the garden.

It is both unwise and disheartening to attempt to care for more garden than can be properly attended to. Comparatively little produce, and usually of inferior quality, will result from an ill-kept garden. Nothing is more dismal and discouraging than a plot of weeds whose vigorous growth has almost completely obliterated all signs of vegetables. A stunted carrot here and there, bullet-like beets, scarcely larger than a marble, a few slender sickly lettuce leaves, these are the rewards of the gardener who permits the weeds to get the better of him.

Weeds will be discussed later, but let everyone who contemplates a vegetable garden take them into consideration and realize that no useful species will grow in competition with weeds, and that it takes time to control their growth. So in making the preliminary decisions as to the size of the garden, full consideration must be given to the time necessary to keep the plot well weeded and otherwise cared for. On the other hand, it is amazing how much a small area of intensely cultivated garden will produce. Always bear in mind that intensive cultivation is more important than extensive cultivation.

The stress upon the necessity of eliminating certain vegetables because of space, and upon the labor required in the care of a garden, should not be discouraging. Actually the results are so satisfying and the yield so substantial that careful gardening is never disappointing. There is no one way which is best. Each garden presents a different problem, and the problem presented is a challenge. There is no satisfaction greater than obtaining the maximum yield from a given plot of land. This book attempts to show how much reward may be expected in the way of results, from a given amount of time spent on a garden of a given size.

As stated, there is no rule-of-thumb as to size. As a working basis, an arbitrary set of conditions must be chosen, and then the amount of seed, yield, labor necessary, etc., established. Each individual will need to vary the amounts and figures given to suit his own particular needs.

An excerpt from *The Garden Encyclopedia*, edited by E. L. D. Seymour, B.S.A., is both pertinent and interesting:

During the World War emergency period it was demonstrated on experimental plots that an abundant supply for one adult person for an entire year can be grown in a space 25 x 30 feet in size, if intensively cultivated, and if the soil is of average fertility. In round figures and with an abundant margin allowance, this means that an acre of ground will produce food for 50 people. The potential value of a subsistence garden to an average family, on which it lays no great burden for planting and maintenance, is therefore evident.

I wish I might say that for purposes of experiment I laid out a unit plot so that I might determine how much in quantity and in what variety that unit would produce. However, the record of my own garden, kept from day to day with some care, should give equivalent information.

As an example, I choose a day at random—August 11th—and list the vegetables gathered that day in succeeding years.

First year:

1 head cabbage
8 bunches celery
1 bunch scallions
9 bunches carrots
8 heads lettuce
4 pounds potatoes
1 peck of peas

Second year:

10 heads lettuce
2 bunches beets
9½ pounds string beans
5 summer squash
1 bunch celery
5 bunches scallions
1 peck Swiss chard
3 cucumbers

This garden has been placed on the same plot of ground for the past ten years, and is now about 100 x 200 feet in area. When first started it was somewhat smaller than this. It produces vegetables not only for our own use, but for a summer population of about fifty people. In addition to the summer use in the 2nd year, about 400 quarts of vegetables were canned for winter use, 5 bushels of onions were laid up, 1 barrel of carrots, 1 bushel of beets, 4 bushels of turnips, 150 bunches of celery, 35 heads of cabbage, and 6 gallons of sauerkraut. There remained in the ground, for use during the winter when conditions permitted and in spring when the ground thawed, at least 5 bushels each of salsify (oyster-plant) and parsnips.

Besides the above stored for winter use, and the fresh vegetables consumed by the family, which through the summer averaged eight people, and vegetables supplied to a summer camp that catered to an average of twenty-two lusty appetites, there was cash income from the sale of surplus vegetables.

The other side of the ledger shows payments for labor, for seeds, for sets, for hen manure, for barn manure, and for nitrates. This left a cash credit in addition to all the house and camp fresh vegetables, plus those that were put by for winter.

My own labor is the only cost not included. My teen-age son, who is away at school and needs the pocket-money, was paid by the hour for all the time he put in on the garden during his summer vacation. My own work in the garden was for the most part done in spare time. It is true that I might have spent those hours whipping the brook trout, or with music; but I have no regrets, and have no feeling that it would be proper to charge my time against the garden as a cost. The garden was a source of deep delight. To watch things grow is a pleasure that far outbalances my labor.

To return to the planning of a garden, we will consider an arbitrary plot which will serve as a basic model for the beginner —to be adjusted to the uses of different-sized families and to differing plot sizes. Inasmuch as my garden is a large one and its harvest is much larger than is required by the needs of the average family, let us reduce it in size and use as our model plot a garden 50 x 75 feet.

Because some species which were profitably grown in the larger garden cannot be grown to best advantage in a plot of this size, the garden we take for our standard will not be just a part of my garden in every detail. There will need to be some adjustments as to amounts planted other than the per cent reduction in size, and there will be a necessary elimination of some species. Actually, however, the latitude the gardener has in deciding what to plant is as wide as the offering of the seed catalogue, limited only by conditions of climate and soil.

In the Appendix will be found convenient reference tables. Among these is a table showing the number of growing days necessary for each variety. As my garden is located in an upland valley in the Green Mountains, where our official average growing season is only ninety days, the choice of species and varieties has been limited to the quickly maturing types. Reference to the table of growing days will enable the user of this book to substitute other, perhaps more desirable, kinds than those I have used. I prefer to speak only from experience and give data only on varieties which I have actually grown.

Here I might say that the conditions which prevail in my locality are perhaps as difficult as in any part of this great country, and if a given vegetable can be grown successfully here, it should be possible to grow it almost anywhere. In twelve years of experience in this locality there have been three years in which we have had three frost-free months, three years in which we have had two frost-free months, three years in which there has been only one month free from frost, and three years in which there has been a frost in every one of the twelve months.

Let us consider the plan for a garden 50 x 75 feet, located in the northeastern part of the United States and adjusted to a short growing season. A brief descriptive list of the vegetables planted, together with the amounts of seeds used, will be found in the Appendix.

CHAPTER II

SOIL

MOST PLANTS CAN be grown without soil; but chemical gardening at the present time is of interest chiefly to the scientist, or to the hobbyist. For the subsistence gardener the soil is the basis, the starting-point of all his efforts.

The soil is the very foundation of life. The earth has been referred to as our mother down through the ages, and with reason, for it is from the soil that all vegetation springs, and all life on the surface of the earth is supported by this vegetation.

Soil is the loose material which covers the surface of the earth and is primarily the result of the disintegration of the rocks which make up the better part of the earth's crust. This disintegration was caused by the action of heat and cold and water upon the rocks. Some of the actions are chemical in nature, and we speak of them as decomposition. The whole process is too complicated to be discussed in detail, having taken place through aeons of time and involving the action of floods and glaciers. We are interested to the extent that the rocks which are basic materials of the soil have a direct bearing on the use of the soil from the gardener's point of view.

There is another factor in the original building of the soil, and that is the placing of the material. This, too, has a bearing on its usefulness for garden purposes. The soil may be either sedentary materials, which remain in the place where they were formed from the original rocks; or transported materials, which have been moved from their place of formation by various agencies. Of the latter there are two types that are of importance to the gardener: the first consists of stream or alluvial deposits, the other of glacial deposits. The alluvial deposits, while not proportionately large, are the more important, for they are

more fertile and will produce the best crops under favorable
conditions.

After the soil has been formed as primary or mineral soil,
further action must occur before it is ready for our use. Further weathering takes place, primitive forms of vegetation appear, followed by more complicated forms. It is this vegetation

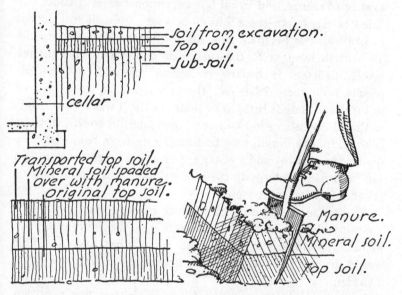

Soil from excavation.
Top soil.
Sub-soil.
cellar
Transported top soil.
Mineral soil spaded
over with manure.
Original top soil.
Manure.
Mineral soil.
Top soil.

DIAGRAM SHOWING MINERAL SOIL
SPREAD ON TOP OF LAND ABOUT NEW
HOUSE FROM CELLAR EXCAVATION.

Figure 1

which really transforms the material covering the earth into
what we know as soil. The decay of the vegetation, resulting in
the building up of organic materials, the action of burrowing
animals and insects, and their dead bodies which add to the
organic content, finally bring the soil to the point where it is
rich and friable and ready for the gardener.

This simple outline of the origin of soil is given so that the
gardener may treat it with understanding and may handle it

to his profit. The making of the soil by nature has taken count-less centuries; the marring of it by man has been a much more rapid process. It is the work of but a few years either to deplete the soil in field or garden or to make it deeper and richer and more productive.

When we choose the site for a garden, we must take the soil as it is, of course, and in all but exceptional cases it is not suf-ficiently fertile. In some instances, even, the soil from cellar excavations has been thrown out and spread over the topsoil. This earth brought to the surface is almost entirely mineral, wholly deficient in humus or organic material, and is com-pletely unfit for garden use. In such a case, if the excavated soil is deep, there is little to be done; but if it was spread thinly so that deep cultivation will reach the topsoil beneath it, there is hope, for the topsoil may be brought up from below by deep spading or plowing and a heavy application of manure or mulch can be turned under with the mineral soil. This should make a reliable soil for garden use.

Another method would be to work manure and humus into the mineral soil, and then spread over it, to the depth of several inches, rich topsoil brought from some other location. This would provide the soil condition necessary for the planting of a garden.

In some instances the soil itself is so shallow that a garden is not practicable. Shallow earth on top of ledge-rock or com-pletely impervious clay would not hold sufficient moisture to permit the successful growing of vegetables.

Ordinarily, however, the plot chosen for the garden site will not be either of mineral earth alone or of shallow soil. Usually there is already some vegetable growth, grass or weeds; and this ground can be made suitable for a garden. It is not always easy, to be sure. In some cases it presents a pretty tough prob-lem, and the transformation cannot be effected in one or even two years. However, the gardener will make the best of the soil he happens to have.

Provided that the drainage is good, the first job is to clear the land. This means the removal of shrubs and stumps, rocks, litter and other debris. But not all sites have perfect drainage. If water stands on the ground in pools for a day or so, the surface drainage is bad. If the ground is boggy and slow to dry out in spring or after storms, the subsoil drainage is bad. In either case the conditions are not conducive to a good garden. Water standing on the soil chills it and excludes the needed air. The result is a soggy sour soil hard to till and unfavorable to most plant growth. In fact, most plants will die if water stands on their roots for any length of time.

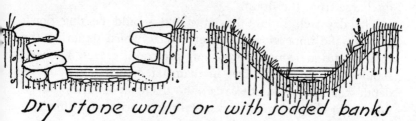

Dry stone walls or with sodded banks

CROSS SECTION
OF DRAINAGE DITCH

Figure 2

Ground on which water does not stand may likewise be sour and heavy; it can be identified by the fact that it is usually covered with moss. The ground is not loose enough, not aerated enough, to be good for garden use.

In neither of these cases, however, is the amount of work necessary to correct the conditions on a small garden plot great. The obvious course would be to locate the garden on gently sloping ground. If this is not possible, and simple grading cannot cure the condition, the gardener must resort to drainage, the garden plot must be ditched.

Common sense will indicate the amount and kind of ditching necessary to procure proper drainage. In some instances an open ditch will serve the purpose; but unless the sides can be laid up with dry-stone masonry they will continually crumble, filling the ditch with sediment. In the absence of stone masonry, a strip two or three feet wide on each side of the ditch should be sodded, and if possible the banks as well. However, the most satisfactory kind of drainage is obtained by using buried drain tile.

All drains, either open or tile, should lead to some spot lower than the garden site, so that the water may run off; and the pitch should be such that there is a continuous fall of at least one inch for each twenty-five feet. If it is not possible to discharge the drain into a lower spot beyond the garden, or into a sewer, a dry well must be dug, into which the water will discharge from the drain.

The dry well should be large and should be dug down through the impervious hardpan or clay which underlies the topsoil, into some more porous soil, preferably gravel. The well should be four or five feet in diameter, depending upon its depth—the shallower, the larger the diameter—and should be filled with cinders, small rocks, or broken brick to within two or three feet of the top; next there should be a layer of straw or cut weeds, and on top of this a layer of clay, well tamped down. The remainder of the hole should then be filled with topsoil, at least a foot deep.

For a garden of the size we have chosen for our model—50 x 75 feet—one ditch or buried tile should afford ample drainage. However, if the ground is exceptionally wet it may be necessary to make the drain V-shaped. If tile is used, be sure to get the hubless, unglazed drainage tile which comes in one-foot lengths. The joints may be covered with tarpaper to prevent dirt from falling through the cracks and plugging it up. The water ordinarily will enter from the cracks at the bottom of the tile, and so will not bring sediment in with it.

Tile should be buried at least twenty inches deep at the shallow end. In other words, if a drain is to run across the garden from one side, through the middle to the other side, the trench should be twenty to twenty-four inches deep at the high edge of the garden, and should run straight, with a smooth bottom and a continuous pitch, so that the ditch at the low edge of the garden is at least twenty-four to twenty-eight inches deep. The tile at the head of the ditch should be protected by a pile of loose stone so that the earth will not enter and fill the pipe.

At the risk of being repetitious, I want to state again that it is of the utmost importance that the soil of the garden be light and well drained. Water-soaked soil is hopeless: it is lumpy and non-friable; it does not get enough air, and as a consequence it turns sour, growing moss and mold. The addition of manure to such soil only tends to heighten the sourness and sogginess; whereas manure added to heavy, well-drained soil will lighten it. Furthermore, heavy wet soil cannot be worked early in the spring. This is a very important factor. To get the soil worked and ready for planting as early as possible is of the utmost importance.

In the matter of drainage I have departed from my resolve to speak only of things which have come to my direct attention in my own garden; for while my garden plot is far from ideal it did not present any very difficult drainage problem. I have laid one line of tile through a soggy end of the garden, and fortunately have no problem of discharge, as the contour of the land permits the water to spread over the ground at a spot some distance from and below the garden. As a result of this experience, however, there is one point which cannot be urged too strongly, and that is that the tile must be at least twenty inches deep, otherwise it is a hazard to tillage. Having made the mistake originally of not laying the drain tile deep enough, I pass my experience on to others, that they may not make the same mistake.

For the guidance of the beginner, I show two working plans for a tile drain, a dry well, and an open ditch.

Now we have a bare expanse of ground, whatever its size may be, cleared of all debris, of all movable rocks and stones; we have the drainage situation well in hand; and in our mind's eye we can already see shining rows of plants, their smooth leaves glinting in the sun.

However, there remains much to be done before the soil is ready to receive the seeds. The nature and amount of the work depend upon the kind of soil and subsoil the garden has. If it so happens that the land to be used is largely made up of alluvial deposit, it is quite probable that the fortunate gardener will have little to do to prepare the soil. It is more likely, however,

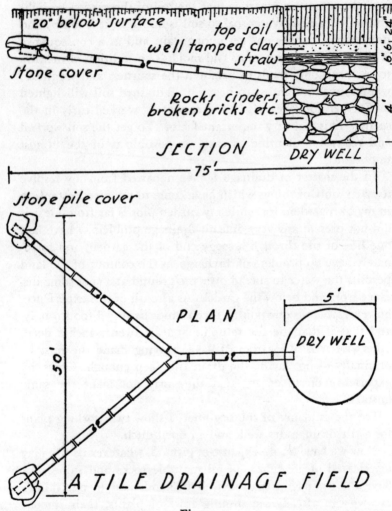

20° below surface

top soil

well tamped clay

straw

6" 6" 24"

Stone cover

Rocks cinders, broken bricks etc.

4'

SECTION

DRY WELL

75'

stone pile cover

PLAN

5'

DRY WELL

50'

A TILE DRAINAGE FIELD

Figure 3

that the soil available will belong to one of the following four classes—although it should be understood that these are generalizations, and that frequently the soil one finds will be a mixture of these classes: (1) Stony loam; (2) sandy loam; (3) light clay loam; (4) heavy clay loam.

Stony loams belong to the geological class of transported soils, and for the most part are glacial in origin. These soils are of mixed characteristics, and can be very productive. But they present a real difficulty to the gardener, for the number of stones is infinite, and their presence makes cultivation difficult. There is but one thing to do, and that is to remove as many of the stones as possible. This will seem an endless job, for each spring the frost will work new stones up to the surface. I have this type of soil in one part of my garden; so do not be discouraged, for the rewards are well worth the labor.

Sandy loams also are apt to be transported soils, and were probably stream deposited. Like stony soils they are mixed in character, and can be very productive. They are marked· by lightness and their inability to hold moisture.

Light clay loams for the most part are residual soils, and are the result of decomposition of sandstones, granite, or gneiss. They are usually acid in reaction. Their physical characteristics are likely to be favorable to gardening, being light and friable without being too porous and dry.

Heavy clay loams are also residual soils and are the result of the decomposition of limestone. They are heavy and clayey and alkaline in reaction. Their heavy nature makes them difficult to work and cultivate. Nevertheless they easily retain their natural fertility, as well as added nutrients; they retain moisture, and they can be made lighter. Properly handled, they can be made to be excellent soils for garden use and will produce fine crops.

It is not possible to judge the quality or fertility of the soil by its color. The color is largely a result of the type of rock from which it is derived. As is well known, however, organic materials tend to give soil a darker color, and their presence is beneficial. Anyone who has ever dug down through the topsoil into the mineral soil which lies beneath has noticed that the top ten or twelve inches are darker than the soil below.

This upper, darker layer, known as topsoil, contains the

organic materials which are essential to the growth of vegetation. The presence of humus in the topsoil not only affords
food for the plants whose roots penetrate it, but it also forms a
sponge, as it were, which retains moisture. Below the topsoil
lies the subsoil, or mineral soil, which is less stocked with
plant nutrients and, being more compacted and almost humus
free, is less able to act as a reservoir for moisture.

The total depth of the soil varies greatly in different localities. I have seen places in Kentucky where, when drilling for
water, the drill point went down through soil to the depth of
at least two hundred feet. Here in Vermont the depth of the
soil varies from a few inches to twenty or thirty feet.

While the roots of few of the vegetables grown in the garden
will penetrate deeper than the topsoil, the depth and kind of
soil beneath it is of interest. If the total depth of the soil is
too little the topsoil will dry out and the vegetables will wither
and die. If the subsoil is compact and clayey or an impervious
hardpan, a drainage problem may result. If the subsoil is too
pervious, on the other hand, both the moisture and the fertility
of the topsoil will leach away through it.

Not only is the nature of the soil of interest to the gardener,
but most emphatically the fertility of the soil as well—the
amount of available plant foods it contains. Other conditions
being equal, the more fertile the soil the more abundant and
vigorous will be the vegetable growth. But the other conditions must be taken into account. For example, a heavy muck
soil, the product of countless generations of vegetable decomposition, would not be ideal soil for the vegetable garden; for,
while rich in humus and nutrients, it is also wet and acid in
reaction. However, if this soil were drained and aerated, and its
acidity neutralized, its high content of available plant foods
would make it ideal for garden use. Indiana's Kankakee bot-
tomlands, once water, are now growing potatoes, and muck-
grown potatoes seem to be superior in every way.

The first test of the fertility of soil is the condition of the
vegetation which grows on it. If the vegetation is lusty and

vigorous the soil is certainly good; if on the other hand the growth is scrawny and scarce, the soil is poor. But however poor the soil may be, it can be improved; and the improvement of the soil is the first consideration of the gardener.

There are, roughly and generally speaking, four classes of poor soil which will require attention before a successful garden can be expected:

(a) Soils which need lightening
(b) Soils which need more body
(c) Acid soils
(d) Soils which need fertilizing

Advice as to the treatment of soils can be had free of charge from any State Department of Agriculture in the Union. I can speak from experience and with authority only about the State in which I live, Vermont. While the practice in this State is, I believe, standard throughout the United States, it is my advice that if any question exists as to the treatment of the soil of any given garden plot, the assistance of the State Department of Agriculture be invoked. A sample of soil, sent in a container which is supplied on request, will be analyzed and a complete report made. The report will define the acidity, or pH, the existence or lack of phosphoric acid, nitrogen and potash, and will include a suggested treatment, in specific terms, for the improvement of the soil. After a couple of years of hit-or-miss methods of soil improvement in my garden, I had the several soils of my plot analyzed, and, acting on the expert advice given, I treated the soil with beneficial results.

Heavy soils can be lightened and improved. The first step, of course, is drainage. If, after satisfactory drainage has been achieved, the soil is still heavy and lumpy, it can be lightened by the addition of sand or ashes. In my father's garden, in which I worked as a boy, the soil was a heavy red clay, and I remember that he used sifted coal ashes from the furnace to lighten it. Coal ashes add a coarse and impervious element to the soil, which loosens and lightens it.

Wood ashes also will lighten the soil, the bits of charcoal and the insoluble ash both tend to make heavy loam more friable. Wood ashes have a fertilizing value as well, for they contain potash. They will be discussed more fully under fertilizers.

Any addition to the humus content of the soil will tend to make it more friable and lighter. Humus can be added by the application of manure, compost, or by plowing under cover-crops. The addition of agricultural lime will aid in the lightening of heavy soils, as well as acting as a neutralizer of acid soils.

Soils which are too light and porous—in other words, which are excessively sandy and will not properly retain moisture—also can be improved. The importance of improving them cannot be overemphasized, for a porous soil will not properly retain any added plant food. Added foods, in the form of commercial fertilizers particularly, will leach away through the soil and their good effects be lost to the vegetable growth which the soil is supporting. Strangely enough, the same procedure which will lighten heavy soils will give body to light soils. The addition of barnyard manure, for instance, will improve soil that is too light and at the same time will enrich it. The addition of humus in any form will give light soil more body.

The garden soil may be too acid; it may be too alkaline. There are many forms of vegetation which prefer soils of acid reaction; others, and this is the larger class, thrive better in soils with an alkaline reaction. A soil analysis by an agricultural laboratory will reveal the exact relative amount of acidity or alkalinity. It is also possible for the soil to be neutral, showing neither acid nor alkaline reaction.

A home-test for determining the acid or alkaline condition of the soil—which I have never used and so cannot guarantee—is to procure some strips of litmus paper from the drugstore. This paper reacts to both acid and alkali. A gray color to begin with, it turns red in the presence of acid, blue in the presence of alkali, and remains gray in a neutral solution. The procedure, then, is to take a bit of soil and shake it up with a little water in a bottle. After the mixture has settled, a strip of litmus paper is inserted and the change in color, if any, observed. This is not a quantitative determination, how-ever, and I question if it can be very useful. The best plan is to have a soil-analysis made.

Because of the fact that the vegetables to be grown react favorably or unfavorably to acid or alkali, it is important that this particular soil condition be understood. Soil acidity is registered in terms of hydrogen ion concentration, which need not concern us here, but for convenience is referred to as pH, and is scaled from 1 to 14, 7 being neutral. A report from the agricultural laboratory will give you results in terms of pH, and thus have more meaning than any home-test. Inasmuch as most plants grow equally well in neutral, mildly alkaline or

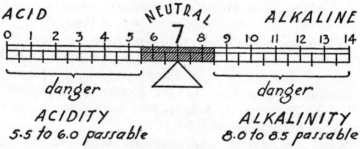

Figure 4

mildly acid soils, acid soils need not cause us concern unless they are highly acid. In other words, if your analysis from the State laboratory shows a pH lower than 6, something must be done to correct the acid condition, for few of the vegetables ordinarily grown will thrive in decidedly acid soil.

Alkaline soil, the opposite of acid soil, is on the other hand more favorable to the growth of most vegetables, and unless the pH reading is higher than 8 there is no cause for concern. Moderately alkaline soil seems beneficial to many of our common garden vegetables; yet except in rare instances soils are more likely to show a slight acid reaction than an alkaline reaction. For this reason it is common and sound practice to treat garden soils with agricultural lime as an agent for lightening heavy soils. Old and exhausted soils, heavy and undrained soils, and soils derived from granite, gneiss and schists are all apt to be acid in reaction, and the addition of agricultural lime is beneficial.

The distinction is made between agricultural lime, mason's lime, and quicklime. Agricultural lime is pulverized limestone rock or calcium carbonate. It is very slowly soluble and its action is mildly alkaline. It will remain in the soil a long while and thus performs valuable work both as a lightener of the soil and as a mild alkali.

Mason's or hydrated lime is calcium hydroxide and is more quickly available as a neutralizer of acid conditions. It is less valuable as a physical agent, while being more valuable as a chemical agent. It is highly recommended for use in the vegetable garden. I have never tried it, however, having used on my own soil the agricultural lime or pulverized limestone.

Quicklime, calcium oxide, should never be used directly on the garden, for it will kill everything with which it comes in contact. Unless the soil is excessively acid the use of agricultural lime is to be recommended, because of its mechanical effect of lightening the soil, its long staying-power, and its power to sweeten the soil.

Wood ashes, also, are alkaline and will neutralize acid soils. Wood ashes contain a great deal of soluble material, of which potash is a valuable plant food. They are therefore of more value as a fertilizer than they are as a soil sweetener. But it is well to remember, when using wood ashes to enrich the soil, that they are alkaline.

The amount of lime to apply to the garden plot should be determined by first having the soil analyzed. I hesitate to give any rule for its application. On my own garden I followed the instructions which accompanied the report of the soil analysis. However, as a rule-of-thumb, a garden 100 feet square, if the soil is heavy and acid, requires from 200 to 300 pounds of agricultural lime.

Just as the proper treatment to give garden soil to change

the pH rating should be on the basis of soil analysis, so, too, should the addition of proper soil nutrients or fertilizers. There are certain characteristics of fertilizer which the gardener should know, and there are practical experiments he can perform which will give the answers to the problem of fertilizing. It is unfortunate that in many localities it is almost impossible to get good barn manure or to get wood ashes, both of which are extremely important to the gardener.

Wood ashes, as has been mentioned, serve to lighten heavy soils, they sweeten acid soils, and they supply available plant food in the form of potash, containing as high as 7 per cent of this substance. They should be spread on the garden in the fall, to be turned under in the spring. Except in cases mentioned in later chapters, their direct application to the plants or as a side dressing is dangerous, for they are likely to burn delicate plant growths. Other valuable uses of wood ashes will be mentioned later.

There are several types of manure, all of them good in their way. The barn manures, cow and horse, are the most common. Sometimes hen manure is available, and sometimes sheep manure can be had. All manures are valuable, used either straight or mixed with various types of bedding, such as hay or straw. Sawdust and shavings are less desirable for manure bedding, for they decompose slowly, and when they are completely decayed they give off acids which are harmful to the soil.

Horse manure, if green, will heat and burn, and for that reason it should not be used until it is well rotted, unless it can be applied fresh and immediately turned under. Cow manure, on the other hand, is cold manure and may be used immediately, conserving valuable liquid ingredients which are thus made available to plant life. It too, however, is best applied well rotted. Poultry manure also will heat and is more concentrated in plant foods than are barn manures; because of these two characteristics, it is wise to mix poultry manure with soil before applying it to the garden. It must be noted also that poultry manure is less bulky and less valuable as a producer of humus than are the barnyard manures. On the other hand, barnyard manures generally contain innumerable seeds, and thus when they are spread on the garden the seeds of countless bothersome weeds are inadvertently spread with them.

Ordinary manures for the most part contain all the elements required to make the soil more fertile and at the same time improve its physical condition. They should be used whenever available, even though the apparent drawbacks, as in the case of weeds, seem to be considerable. Barn manures should be applied in the fall, if possible, as they decompose slowly; they may be applied as thick as four or five inches.

Humus, the organic material found in topsoil, is necessary for garden growth, both for its food value and its action as a sponge in retaining moisture. It is made up of decayed vegetation and, to a smaller extent, decayed animal material and bacteria. The building up of the decayed vegetable materials is a result of the death of successive generations of vegetable growth, beginning with the primitive forms such as lichens and mosses which first cover the bare rock and mineral soil; while the animal matter is the result of the death of countless generations of insects and animals, all down the list to microscopic organisms. Without humus, soil would be dead and inert, wholly incapable of growing vegetables. Besides being a plant food and a medium for retaining water, humus aids the growth of bacteria which are necessary for the breaking down of the soil minerals so that they may become available as plant food.

These functions are of the utmost importance, and so every means possible must be taken to maintain the humus content of the garden soil. Manure of any kind is of prime importance as a supplier of humus. But manure is often hard to procure, and when it is not possible to get it in sufficient amounts, it is necessary to provide other substances which will supply our garden soil with humus. These sources are the compost pile; green cover or forage crops plowed under; and purchasable forms, such as peat moss and muck.

The compost pile is the most practical and the easiest method, unless manure can be had, to supply the garden soil with humus. Right here I must confess that I am far from proud of my own compost pile; but perhaps my mistakes and carelessness may at least act as a guide to what not to do. And possibly I may be excused on the ground that I have no difficulty in obtaining all the well-rotted barnyard manure that I need, at so slight a cost it does not pay me to spend much time on the

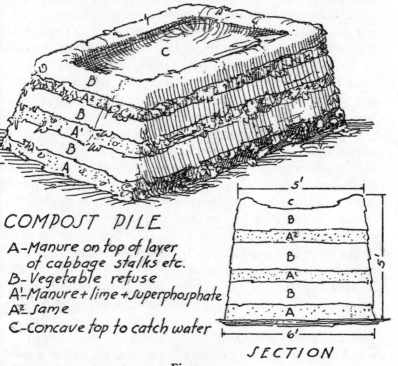

COMPOST PILE

A-Manure on top of layer
   of cabbage stalks etc.
B-Vegetable refuse
A¹-Manure + lime + superphosphate
A²-same
C-Concave top to catch water

SECTION

Figure 5

compost pile. In fact, I keep one solely because I cannot bear to see valuable humus builders thrown away and lost. Were I dependent upon my compost pile for humus, I would be more careful in caring for it.

According to the best authorities, a compost pile should be built up in a rectangular shape, rather longer than wide, so that all parts may be accessible from the sides. It should not be more than five or six feet wide, and may be as long as needed.

The height is determined by convenience and the amount of material available, but it should not be over five feet. It should be built in layers, and it should be treated as it is built with commercial fertilizers and should be carefully kept moist.

The first layer, about six inches deep, should be of some heavy coarse material such as sods, broken-up cornstalks, cabbage-stalks, etc.; next come successive layers of any vegetable refuse available—lawn clippings, leaves, weeds from the garden, any green material, in fact, which is reasonably free from plant diseases. Each layer of vegetable refuse, as it is added, should be sprinkled with a commercial fertilizer which contains all three of the basic plant foods—phosphorus, potash and nitrogen. But an occasional sprinkling of agricultural lime should be substituted for the fertilizer as the pile grows.

If possible, the layers of vegetable refuse should alternate with layers of manure. In any case, the top layer should be kept slightly concave, or hollowed out, so that water will collect when it rains. If the weather is dry the pile should be wet down with the garden hose. Moisture is necessary for decay and the compost is not ready for use until it is well decayed.

If the pile can be built all at one time, which is not ordinarily the case, the whole can be spaded over and re-piled in the same shape after two or three months. This will put the decayed material on top and the undecayed material underneath, where the process of decomposition will take place more rapidly. If the pile is built up slowly over a period of time, it will require much longer for it to become decayed enough for use. As the bottom decomposes, however, the pile can be spaded over, and the new layers be added, until the whole is decomposed and ready for use.

Compost can be used on the garden just as it is dug from the heap. It is applied as one would apply manure. It will not burn or injure plants and it will supply them with valuable foods, while at the same time it improves the condition of the soil, making it more friable and more able to retain moisture.

Another substitute for barnyard manure is the cover-crop or green manure—a crop which is planted and grown only to be

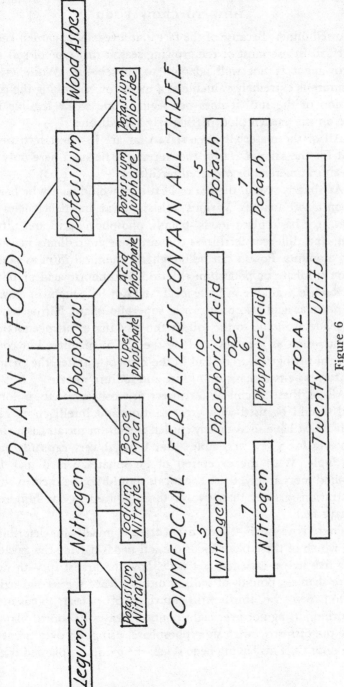

Figure 6

plowed under. Because of the fact that a vegetable garden keeps the soil in use most of the growing season this type of soil improvement is not well adapted to garden use. While green manure is extremely valuable as a means of improving the condition of the soil, it does not seem to me to be feasible for use on the garden plot, particularly a small one.

All of the materials discussed so far are in effect fertilizers; but for the sake of clarity that term will be used here only to mean commercial or prepared fertilizers.

As already stated, the use of fertilizers would wisely be based upon a soil analysis. Various soils show varying deficiencies in the three basic plant foods—potash, phosphoric acid and nitrogen; and different fertilizers contain these ingredients in varying amounts. Potash can be bought in chemical form as potassium sulphate or potassium chloride. Phosphoric acid or phosphates are available in bone-meal, and can be bought in chemical form as acid phosphate, or as superphosphate. Nitrogen can be made available to the soil by the growing of nitrogen-fixing plants, such as legumes, and by the use of manure; but commercial nitrogen is to be had in the form of nitrates, the chemical forms being potassium nitrate and sodium nitrate.

All of these chemical fertilizers are concentrated in form and should be used with great caution and intelligence. The only one I have used on my garden is sodium nitrate, as a side dressing for a few vegetables, and I use it very carefully and sparingly. With the exception of phosphates, which may be applied more freely, these chemicals should not be used in concentrations greater than two or three pounds to one hundred square feet.

There is a system—I have never tried it myself—for determining which of these plant foods the soil needs. Divide the garden into five strips, each ten feet wide. Sow the first strip with not more than six pounds of sodium nitrate; leave the second strip blank; sow the third with muriate of potash (potassium chloride), using not over eight pounds. Leave the fourth blank. Sow the fifth strip with superphosphate, using not over twenty-five pounds. This having been done, the garden is planted with the rows running at right angles to the strips of chemicals as sown. The result of growth will give the gardener some idea as to which of the three the garden most needs; there may even be an indication that all three are needed. I repeat that I have not tried this experiment, as interesting as it would be; and I strongly recommend the more direct course—have the soil analyzed and then treat it as the laboratory experts advise.

Commercial fertilizers come in various combinations of the three essential ingredients; and while a gardener might carry out the experiment as outlined, and thus mix his own fertilizer based upon the result, it is easier and less disagreeable to buy ready-mixed fertilizers. All standard brands are reliable, and the guaranteed analysis is printed on each bag. The things to look for are the three necessary elements, nitrogen, phosphoric acid and potash. It is common practice to put up commercial fertilizers so that they contain a total of 20 "units." These units are printed on the bag, and the fertilizer is referred to as, say, a 5-10-5 fertilizer, meaning that the percentages of available nitrogen, phosphoric acid and potash are respectively five, ten and five. The report and recommendation from the State laboratory after having tested any given soil, will tell you what type of commercial fertilizer should be used.

In using commercial fertilizers, care should be taken not to apply them too heavily. Small, frequent applications are better than occasional heavy ones. Furthermore, they should not be allowed to come into direct contact with the plants.

Soil must of course be cultivated before it is ready to receive the seeds; but first it must be put into proper condition for cultivation. It has been the intent of this chapter to act as a guide in the preparation of the soil.

CHAPTER III

PLANTING THE GARDEN

HAVING PREPARED THE garden spot, we are ready for the next step. In gardening there are four main steps: (1) Preparing the soil; (2) planning the physical layout of the garden, including the amounts of each vegetable, the rotation of crops, and cover-cropping, if any; (3) the growing of the garden, which includes the control of diseases and weeds, the cultivation and feeding; and (4) the harvesting of the crop, including the care and storage and canning of the vegetables.

Where a new garden is being started, the first step is the most important of all. None of the others can be carried to a completely successful conclusion unless the first step has been well done. And the first step must be repeated each succeeding year. No soil can be brought to the proper conditions in one year's use. In vegetable gardens the soil improves with use. After ten years the garden plot I am using now is still improving.

All the preliminary work of preparing the garden plot—clearing, ditching, grading, manuring—should be done the season before planting, so that when spring comes and the soil is sufficiently dry the spading and plowing can be started immediately. If the garden is not too large it is better to spade and fork it than to have it plowed. This is for two reasons. First, the portion of the garden which is to receive the seeds to be planted first can be spaded, prepared, and seeded; then another section can be prepared for the seeds which are to be planted next. In this way, in installments as it were, each piece is fresh and moist for the seeding. Otherwise the part of the garden last to be planted is likely to be dried out and compacted by tramping over it.

The second reason is that spading by hand, if carefully done, does a better job of turning over the soil and breaking up the lumps. Any rocks located while spading can be removed, whereas a plow might jump over them and cover them up again. However, a plot 50 x 75 feet is quite a big piece to turn over by hand, and it is fair to assume that in some cases it will be wisest to have it plowed. My garden is large enough so that I spade by hand one quarter-section—a plot approximately 50 x 100. This receives the early plantings, and later the balance of the garden is plowed.

Whenever it is possible it is a good idea to do most of this preparing of the soil in the fall. There is usually a slack period then and time can be found more conveniently to work the soil than in the spring. Also, the action of frost and melting snows on the soil will help to break it up further and kill harmful organisms.

Of course, it is not possible to do this work in the fall where crops are left in the ground. I always leave some parsnips and salsify for use in the spring. The table value of these two vegetables, early in the spring as soon as departing frost permits them to be dug, cannot be overestimated in this climate where the winter is seven months long. There are some varieties of other vegetables—such as brussels-sprouts, celery, cabbage, broccoli, parsley, kale and turnips—that are not hurt by frost. Some, indeed, are improved by frost; and brussels-sprouts will stand a hard freeze. The value of these vegetables in the garden in the off-season far outweighs the benefits gained by fall cultivation, so they are always left in the ground until it freezes; and it is then too late to cultivate.

If the garden plot is a new one, about to serve its first year as a contributor to the family income, the soil will need more working than will be necessary later on. If it is of greensward— that is, if it is growing grass—it should be plowed in the fall so that the sods will have a chance to disintegrate and break up under the action of frost and weather. The plowed land should then in the spring be harrowed with a disk harrow, repeatedly, in both directions, across and around, so that as much loose soil is worked up as is possible. But no matter how much of the preliminary work, the plowing and harrowing, is done by machines, the last, the final putting into shape, will have to be done by hand if the best results are to be obtained.

This final whipping into shape can be done in any number of different ways. The system which I find the most satisfactory is to lay out the amount of ground to be planted. Then I go over it very carefully with a potato-hook, working backward, so that my footprints are gone over as the work pro-

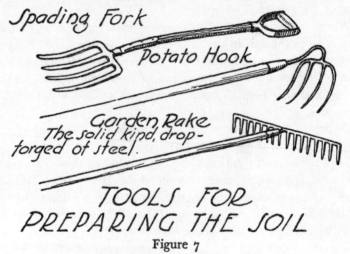

Spading Fork

Potato Hook

Garden Rake
The solid kind, drop-
forged of steel.

TOOLS FOR PREPARING THE SOIL

Figure 7

ceeds. This should be done carefully. All stones that will not slip through the tines of the fork should be removed; all large lumps of soil should be broken; and the cultivation should be as deep as strength and the tines of the fork permit. After this is done, the next step is to go over it all again in the same manner, this time using a steel garden rake. This second cultivation will remove all the smaller debris, clods, stones, etc., and will break up all the lumps missed by the first treatment. It will leave the soil finely broken up and mellow, ready for the seed.

Another operation of soil preparation—which I have not found it necessary to use in my garden—should be described. This is known as "trenching" and is used to break up the subsoil and thus improve drainage and eventually deepen the topsoil. Trenching should be **done** in the fall. Beginning at one side of the garden, the topsoil is shoveled aside and piled. This removing of the topsoil leaves a trench about two or three feet wide, the length of the garden, with the subsoil exposed. This strip of subsoil is then spaded as deeply as possible with a spading-fork and humus is added. The topsoil of an adjoining strip is next removed and thrown into the first trench; and that exposed subsoil is spaded. Thus the topsoil of the second strip

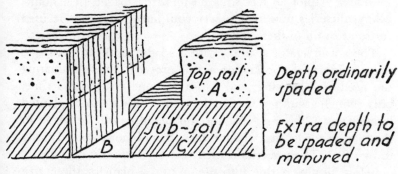

Top soil "A" spaded and thrown in trench "B"
Sub-soil "C" then spaded and thrown on top
of "A" and so forth.

TRENCHING.

Figure 8

becomes the topsoil of the first strip. Proceeding thus across the garden, the last trench is filled with the topsoil of the first strip by carting the pile across the garden in a wheelbarrow.

This operation of trenching is a valuable one, particularly where the subsoil is hard and impervious. The importance of the depth of soil preparation cannot be exaggerated. The long smooth symmetrical carrots and parsnips which are pictured in the seed catalogues are not the result of any magic formula. They are the natural growth of healthy seeds of standard varieties grown in deep mellow soil.

Now to consider what one might expect in the way of labor

or expense, if the labor is hired, to prepare the garden for seeding—assuming that the ground is in readiness to be prepared for planting. If farm machinery and labor are available a plot of land 50 x 75 feet can be plowed, harrowed, and dragged in a short time, and at a modest cost. If the gardener wishes to spade by hand, or is required to do so by lack of available machinery, the total time required to spade such a plot should not be over 24 hours. A plot 25 feet square should be spaded in 4 hours. Many nurseries now rent power equipment that can be used for some or all of these tasks.

The advantage of spading with a spading-fork, to repeat, is that the lumps are broken up as one proceeds, thus eliminating the need of harrowing; and it can be done a little at a time, only enough ground to receive the seeds which are to be planted immediately. This first spading and planting will be made in that part of the garden which is most free of moisture and ready to be tilled. The varieties chosen will be frost-resistant ones.

Before sinking a tine into the ground a plan for the entire garden should be outlined on paper. This should be done in the winter, long before the actual work of gardening can begin. This plan is the backbone of the whole garden operation, and it must be made even before the seeds can be ordered; for after the plan is in definite shape we know precisely the varieties and the amounts of seeds to buy. This done, and the weather permitting, a start can be made on the actual work. But first, the plan.

Our garden plot is, let us say, 50 x 75 feet, on a southeastern exposure with the length of the garden running up and down the slope. We should like to have the rows run north and south, so that the summer sun, moving from east to west, will shine on both sides of the plants. But a more important consideration than sunshine on both sides of the rows is that of water run-off. The rows must always run across the slope, forming a series of little dams to hold back the water, which in summer frequently falls in deluges. If the rows run with the slope, they form channels through which the water courses; the loose soil of the garden between the rows is consequently washed away and the roots of the plants exposed. Worse than this, the life-blood of the garden, the rich topsoil, is washed away and lost, being deposited perhaps in the ditch, the brook, or in the sewer.

Next comes the question of spacing the rows. For convenience in planting, the fewer variations in spacing the better. Furthermore, and this may be heresy, the closer together the rows can be, the better. There are two good reasons for this. The first and more obvious is that more vegetables can be produced from a given amount of land; the second is that close rows require less cultivation, for the growing plants more completely shade the earth between the rows, and this gives the weeds less chance to thrive and prosper. The method of cultivation, however, is a factor in determining the spacing; gardens which are to be cultivated by horse-drawn implements must have the rows far enough apart to permit of such cultivation.

For a garden of the size we are about to lay out, hand cultivation is preferable. Keeping the number of variations in spacing down to the minimum, there are six different measurements which I use in my garden. All the smaller vegetables are placed in rows one foot apart; corn and bush beans two feet apart; peas in double rows with three feet between them, with the tall peas five feet apart. Broccoli and cabbage, etc., will be in rows two and a half feet apart. This will be discussed in detail later. It is shown on the plot plan facing page 1.

The first step now, if it was not done in the winter, is to procure a sheet of smooth brown wrapping-paper about 24 x 30 inches. On this will be drawn to scale the plan of the garden, showing the number of rows, the distance apart, the variety or varieties in each row, and indicating the succession of crops.

It is absolutely necessary to have a plan of the garden to get the most out of your time, your money, and your soil. For the first few years of vegetable growing I followed the common country practice of going to the general store in the spring, where I would look over the selection of packaged seeds displayed in the racks. I would pick one here and one there, guessing as to the amounts wanted and deciding on the spur of the moment as to the variety. As a result, the garden was a hit-or-miss affair, with seeds left over in some cases and serious shortages of some vegetables in others. Using a plan, however, there is nothing left to chance. The size of the plot is known, the varieties and amounts can be decided in advance, and the seeds purchased to fill the requirements.

Having acquired a suitable sheet of paper, tack it down on a piece of plywood or wallboard. Get your pencil and a ruler, or better still a ¼-inch scale; but an ordinary ruler will serve the purpose admirably. For each foot of garden lay off ¼ inch on the ruler, and for each six inches lay off ⅛ inch; in other words, 1 inch equals 4 feet. Now draw the garden plot to scale —if the plot is 50 feet by 75, it will be shown on the paper as a rectangle 12½ inches wide and 17¾ inches long. With the garden outline finished, next draw the lines which will indicate the rows and the hills.

The actual drawing of the plan, the laying out of the garden, will be the result of experience. Experience alone will tell which varieties are most successful, which the family likes best, and what the family needs are. The garden plan will never be a static thing. As a garden history is built up, the plan will gradually change, and these changes will be the result of constant experimentation.

The plan offered here is for the gardener who is just beginning, with the belief that while it cannot be completely satisfactory to anyone, it may perhaps give the beginner a fair start. It may save him many mistakes, much hit-or-miss experimenting. The plan is an approximate quarter-reduction of my own garden of the last year. The varieties are ones suited to the New England climate and the choices in all instances are of quick-maturing varieties. In order that the beginner may modify this plan to suit his own requirements of soil and climate, I have inserted in the Appendix charts showing:

    (a) Amount of seed necessary for 100 feet
    (b) Proper spacing of rows and plants
    (c) Number of seeds per ounce
    (d) Amount of seeds for given number of plants

    (e) Dates for planting
    (f) Depth for planting
    (g) Days to harvest
    (h) Fertilizer, lime chart

The first decision to be made, in this plan of the garden, is the kind of vegetables to be grown. I have chosen for the list: lettuce, radishes, salsify (oyster-plant), onions, Swiss chard, summer squash, cucumbers, corn, beets, carrots, cabbage, tomatoes, cauliflower or broccoli, limabeans, two varieties of shell beans, two varieties of snapbeans, early peas, late peas, spinach, endive, and parsley.

The next decision is the amount of each. This is the most difficult part of the whole job, for it is as bad to have vegetables go to waste as it is to have a shortage, to have a surplus of vegetables you've grown tired of and only enough of others to tantalize. This choice in particular is the result of experience. The amounts given on the present plan represent a compromise between several factors—space, taste, usefulness, and probable consumption; space of course being the most important. Some vegetables, as we know, must be eliminated because of space. There are no potatoes, winter squash, canteloupes, pumpkins, brussels-sprouts or celery included in our plan; yet I grow all of these in my larger garden. There are fewer rows of corn, peas, cauliflower and onions than might be used.

In laying out a garden, much valuable information can be acquired from the United States Department of Agriculture and from the departments of agriculture in each of the states. This information is available at little or no cost and is constantly being updated. Because of changing conditions, varieties of vegetables go in and out of favor. In addition, methods of controlling insects and diseases are constantly being improved. It is suggested that the most up-to-date information be secured at the beginning of each year.

In laying out this plan I have assumed that the plot slopes gently from north to south, and that the soil at the upper or north end dries out sooner than that at the other end. For that reason those vegetables which can go in earliest and which are not harmed by frost are planted in the first rows; for here the ground is in condition to be spaded and worked first. On the other hand, peas, which prefer a soil that remains moist, are put in at the lower end of the garden, and this as soon as the ground can be properly prepared. Spinach is planted between the rows of peas; for spinach, too, prefers the moister soil, and will be used and out of the way before the peas are so high that they shade the plants unduly.

The row of early peas will be pulled and vines placed on the compost pile as soon as bearing is finished. The space occupied by them will then be planted to late cabbage sets, or as suggested on this plan.

The tall later peas will also be removed when they have ceased bearing, and the space they occupied will be planted to two more rows of spinach. There will be room here for a row of endive and a row of Swiss chard as well; both thrive in the late summer and resist frost, and will supply greens and salads right up to the hard freezes and snow.

The parsnip and parsley rows are also planted to radishes. The radishes come up within a few days and will mark the rows, for both parsley and parsnip seeds take a long while to germinate, sometimes several weeks. This is important, for unless the rows are visible it is impossible to cultivate them properly; and by the time the parsley and parsnip rows would be showing, the weeds would have such a start that it would be a tough job to get them under control.

The first planting of lettuce can be used from the very beginning, as the thinnings of the row, even though small and a chore to wash for the table, are delicious. As the row is used, more lettuce can be planted for a later crop, or radishes if you prefer.

Let us consider each of the vegetables suggested for this

garden—the variety used and the reason for selecting it, cultivation hints, diseases and pests and their control, and culture notes in general. It must be remembered that the choice of species and varieties made here is by no means final. Other varieties may be chosen, and other kinds of vegetables. The

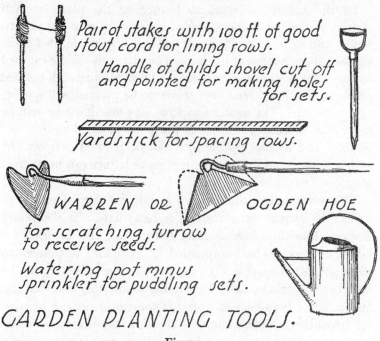

Pair of stakes with 100 ft. of good stout cord for lining rows.

Handle of childs shovel cut off and pointed for making holes for sets.

Yardstick for spacing rows.

WARREN OR OGDEN HOE

for scratching furrow to receive seeds.

Watering pot minus sprinkler for puddling sets.

GARDEN PLANTING TOOLS.

Figure 9

seed catalogues and standard reference books will give specific information about those that are not included here. The scope of this handbook will not permit the inclusion of all species nor the discussion of all varieties of each species.

LETTUCE

Lettuce is frost-resistant to a certain extent and can be planted ordinarily as early as May 1st. In this climate, however, in upland Vermont, the soil cannot be prepared as early as that, and I generally get my seed in about the last week in May.

Lettuce requires rich well-prepared soil and should be planted very shallow, not over one-fourth inch deep. The row should be patted and firmed down with the hand after the seeds have been covered. The seeds are very small and light and it is difficult to scatter them other than rather thickly.

Of the half-row allotted to lettuce on the plan, one-half should be planted to *Black Seeded Simpson,* a loose-leaf variety, tender and delicate, much better flavored than the headed varieties which are bought at the store. The plants should be thinned to stand two or three inches apart, and the thinnings can be used on the table. The twelve feet of row to be planted will require very little seed. The smallest package, one-fourth ounce, will be more than sufficient, for it will plant about one hundred feet of row. The balance of the seed can be planted between the early cabbage, and if it is so desired more lettuce can be planted after the early cabbage is used.

The other half of the half-row should be planted to a head variety of lettuce. An early tender head lettuce is the *White Boston*. The thinnings of head lettuce can also be used for salads, or they can be transplanted. They should be thinned to stand six inches apart in the row, and the transplants should be set out six inches apart. Depending upon the tastes of the family, space between cabbages and tomato plants can be used for transplants. Furthermore, by the time the plants are ready to set out, the half-row of radishes will be gone, and this space can be used for lettuce transplants.

Lettuce is best when grown rapidly, and therefore, since nitrogen promotes leaf growth, it will pay to side dress sparingly with sodium nitrate. This fertilizer is a white granulated substance and should not come in contact with the plants. It should be sown alongside of the row, two or three inches away, on the uphill side, scattered sparingly through the fingers. It can be applied once or twice during the growing season.

Fortunately, lettuce is not particularly subject to diseases or the ravages of insects, for by its very nature it would be dangerous to spray with poison. If disease does appear, destroy the affected plants, and be sure to plant your seeds in a new spot in the garden another year.

ONIONS

Onions can be raised from seeds or from sets. Onion sets are small dried onions, grown especially for planting in the garden. For the past three years I have used no sets, as I have had no trouble raising large, well-matured onions from seeds even in our short growing season. There are two objections to sets— first, the cost, and second, the fact that they may bring disease or pests to your garden.

Onions in the vegetable garden serve a triple purpose. They are delicious as greens or scallions, and the thinnings can be used in this way with great pleasure; they are an excellent table vegetable boiled or creamed, from the size of a walnut to maturity; and the mature onion, dried, can be kept and used all winter long.

The seeds of onions can be sown just as early in the spring as the ground can be worked. They should be planted early so that the shallow-rooted seedlings will not dry out, and the bulbs will have ample time to mature. They should be planted in rich, well-worked, well-broken-up soil, but they do better in moist soil than in dry. In fact, late-planted onions are likely to fail because of the dryness. The seeds, small and black, are difficult to plant sparingly, but they should be sown as thinly as possible to save back-breaking labor in thinning later. They should be covered one-half inch deep and should be lightly tamped down after planting.

It is very important that onions be thinned to three or four inches apart, and that they be frequently cultivated and kept free of weeds. When the bulbs begin to swell out and ripen, the tops should be broken over, either by hand or by a light roller, such as an empty barrel, so that the tops will die. Some thick-necked onions will never mature, for the growth goes up the stalk; they will not keep, and should be the ones selected for table use while green. After the tops have all died, the **onions** should be pulled and, unless the weather is rainy, should be left out on the ground for a day or two to dry out. If they must be pulled in bad weather, they may be taken indoors and then, when fair weather comes, spread on a canvas in the sun to dry. They should be stored loosely in slatted crates so that the air can get to them freely.

Virtually all members of the onion group can be grown in a variety of soils. Some of them can be grown at one time of the year or another in any part of the country that has fertile soil and ample moisture. They require but little garden space to produce enough for a family's needs.

One-half ounce of seeds will plant two fifty-foot rows; a half-ounce packet of each variety is recommended. The average percent of germination of onion seeds is quite low, so it is important that the best seeds be bought. In fact, this is a sound principle to follow in the purchase of any seeds. Buy all your seeds well in advance from one reliable dealer, and continue to purchase from him until you can find someone else who is producing better seeds. For the past four years I have bought seeds from the Eastern States Farmers' Exchange and have had better success with their seeds than with any others that I have ever used.

The enemies of the onion are several, the worst being the maggot. Another insect pest is onion thrips. The diseases are downy mildew, purple blotch, blast, smut, and pink root. The first three diseases can be controlled by applications of zineb or maneb. Smut and pink root cannot be easily controlled and it is best not to plant in soil where these diseases have occurred.

Thrips, which blanch and deform the leaves, can be controlled by spraying with malathion. Plants should be examined for thrips when they are 4 to 6 inches high. The recommended mixture of a 25% wettable powder formulation is one level tablespoon malathion to one gallon of water. The maggot, in my opinion, is the worst enemy of all, for it not only attacks onions but it spreads from them throughout the garden, attacking all the crucifers—members of the Mustard Family, which includes radishes, turnips, cabbages, cauliflower, broccoli and brussels-sprouts.

The maggot is a small white worm, the larva of a small fly. The fly lays its eggs in the soil at the base of the plants, and then the hatched maggots burrow into the bulb of the onion. If they get started early they will kill the young plants, but if the bulbs are well formed the plants may survive, but the onions will be spoiled. This pest, if not controlled, can completely ruin your onions, and once started the eggs will remain in the soil and carry over from year to year. Worse, the maggots will travel from onions to cabbages first, then to cauliflower, then to radishes and eventually to turnips. They will completely kill cabbages and cauliflower and will ruin the radishes. Any onion plant which looks sickly and begins to wilt and droop should be pulled and examined for maggots.

The recommended control for maggots is, again, malathion. This should be mixed in the same proportion as indicated for thrips. Plants should be sprayed three times in seven-day intervals when leaves emerge. Saturate soil with spray near stems. All pesticides should be used with great care. Be sure to read and understand all container label instructions. Wash immediately any part of the body exposed to insecticide and call a doctor immediately if sickness occurs shortly after using insecticide.

My own control for maggots, and the one I recommend, is not given by any of the accepted authorities, but I can testify to its effectiveness. Two years ago my garden was plagued with maggots and I frantically used the various recommended solutions with poor effect. Last year I took the advice of an old greenhouse expert and as a result had a garden completely free from maggots. The control is simply to use wood ashes.

In the case of onions, when the plants are well up, say four or five inches high—and this should be before the fly lays its eggs—sprinkle wood ashes freely along the row so that the soil around each plant is covered. The wood ashes will not burn the onions and they will effectively prevent the fly from laying its eggs wherever the ashes are scattered. Furthermore, the wood ashes are beneficial to the growth of the onions, as well as being a valuable pest control.

RADISHES

Radishes have one outstanding characteristic which recommends them to everyone, especially to children who plant gardens. They can practically always be counted on to grow. Sow radish seeds almost anywhere and you get radishes, and that promptly. Many people enjoy them as a table relish; and they are among the first fruits of the garden—under favorable conditions they are ready to be pulled and eaten within three weeks of planting.

Radishes can be planted just as early as the soil can be worked in the spring. The seeds can be scattered in the row so that thinning is not necessary if the job is done with care. The plants should be one to two inches apart in the row; and the rows twelve inches apart. On the plan radishes have been indicated as row markers for parsley and parsnips, which are both slow to germinate. These seeds should be scattered only to the extent that the young plants will come up in sufficient quantity to mark the rows. In addition the plan calls for one half-row. The seeds are planted one-half inch deep in almost any kind of soil. The better worked and richer the soil, the more quickly the radishes will grow and the finer flavor they will have. The *Early Scarlet Globe* is the variety recommended. Using radishes as a marker crop in addition to the half-row will require the purchase of one-half ounce of seeds, and this should cost only twenty-five or at most fifty cents for this small packet of seeds.

As for their diseases or pests, I have never seen any except the white maggot, and ordinarily if planted early the radishes will mature before the eggs have a chance to hatch. If trouble is experienced with late radishes, I feel sure that the application of wood ashes will prove to be an effective control, although I have not had occasion to use ashes on radishes myself.

PARSNIPS

While there are many people who do not like parsnips any too well, including myself, they should be given room in the garden for their one outstanding characteristic: they actually improve in flavor if left in the ground over the winter, no mat ter how deep the frost or how cold the weather. Thus they afford a fresh vegetable for the table in the early spring when fresh vegetables are most acceptable. Furthermore, they are highly palatable when made into a thick cream soup. They can be used as late in the fall as the condition of the ground will permit them to be dug, and then again in the spring as soon as the ground thaws enough to dig them, for as long as the tops remain unsprouted.

Parsnips should grow in deep topsoil to produce the desirable clean straight roots. Rich soil, prepared with finely broken well-rotted manure, and spaded at least a foot deep, is ideal. The seeds should be planted one-half inch deep, in rows twelve inches apart, and the earth should be lightly tamped after planting. The plants should be thinned to stand two to three inches apart.

The variety recommended is the *Improved Hollow Crown*. The smallest packet of seeds, one-half ounce, will supply enough for one hundred feet of row, much more than is needed.

No diseases or pests have ever attacked parsnips in my garden, and it is not likely that the gardener of a small plot, the subsistence type of garden, will be faced with a serious parsnip pest or disease problem.

SALSIFY

Salsify—or oyster-plant, as many people call it—although not a popular green-grocer vegetable, is useful to the home garden for the same reason that parsnips are. The roots grow slowly, as do parsnips, and they can be left in the ground over winter, actually improving with freezing.

The directions for planting parsnips are to be followed for

salsify. Both are satisfactory crops to grow, for if planted in deep friable soil they can be counted on to produce an ample supply of good roots. One-half ounce of salsify seeds will be sufficient to plant fifty feet of row. The variety recommended is the *Red Sandwich Island.*

Besides supplying a welcome spring vegetable, another attractive feature to the home gardener is that salsify is free from enemies. I have had no pests of any kind bother salsify in my garden.

PARSLEY

A little parsley goes a long way, but it seems reasonable to devote half a row to this easily grown vegetable which is so useful as a garnish and a seasoning. It can be left in the ground till well after the first frosts, and unless the winter is severe it will sometimes remain green until spring, when the time comes to prepare the garden soil for the seeds of the new season.

Because parsley seeds germinate very slowly, a marker crop of radishes should be planted with them. The seeds should be sown one-fourth inch deep and the earth lightly tamped over them after planting. The soil should be fertile, and the rows twelve inches apart. The young plants need not be thinned if the seeds are scattered in the row as sparingly as possible. Parsley is slow in growing and will not be ready to use for perhaps three months.

Enemies rarely molest parsley; none have ever reared their ugly heads in my garden.

TURNIPS

The other half of the parsley row can well be planted to turnips. While these sturdy roots do not have any real place in a backyard garden, at least they serve the table with a distinctive vegetable which can be stored; and the thinnings in the early spring make very acceptable greens.

Turnips can be planted as early in spring as the soil can be prepared. They should be sown sparingly and the plants thinned to six or eight inches apart; the thinnings, as has been mentioned, are delicious as boiled greens. Turnips do well in almost any soil, and should be planted in rows twelve inches apart.

The rutabaga, or Swedish turnip, may be used instead of the regular turnip, if preferred. It grows larger and the roots are more fibrous, but if used when small and before the texture becomes stringy, the rutabaga makes, in the opinion of many people, a more acceptable vegetable for table use than does the regular turnip, the flesh being yellow, firm, sweet and tender. If the rutabaga is planted the crop will be slower to mature, not being ready for the table for about three months after planting, in contrast to the two months which should suffice to mature turnips.

In either case the seeds should be sown one-half inch deep, on moist soil, and firmed over after planting; one-fourth ounce of seeds will be more than sufficient to plant the half-row. A popular white-fleshed variety is *Purple Top White Globe*. If rutabaga is preferred, popular varieties are *American Purple Top* (yellow-fleshed) or *Sweet German* (white-fleshed).

The enemies of the turnip are the same as those of all the crucifers, and their name is legion. The ones most likely to be encountered are leaf-hoppers and maggots; and club-root, a bacterial disease. Of the three I have experienced only the first two in my garden. I have had club-root attack the other crucifers, cabbage and cauliflower in particular, but never the turnip. In any event, experiences in the past year have shown that in the case of the cabbage and cauliflower, the wood-ashes treatment effectively controls both club-root and maggots.

It seems as if the last vegetable on the maggot's menu is the turnip, and I doubt very much if one half-row of turnips in the home garden will offer any problem in the control of either maggots or club-root. The leaf-hopper, on the other hand, is almost certain to be present. To control this I successfully used a commercial dust insecticide containing among other things rotenone. The use of this and other insecticides will be spoken of in more detail in another chapter.

CARROTS

Carrots, often referred to disdainfully as "rabbit food," came into nationwide prominence as an item of war defense during World War II. Carrots contain carotin, a yellow pigment that is transformed by the body into vitamin A, which helps to insure sharp human vision at night. Hence, carrots were fed to the flyers of the Army and Navy. Fish-liver oils, the other chief source of vitamin A at that time, were in scarce supply following the outbreak of war in 1939.

Carrots are a valuable table vegetable, delicious either raw as a relish or cooked as a vegetable. What would a pot-roast be without carrots? Or a stew? They can be used from the very first when the pencil-sized thinnings can be served raw as a salad or relish; then later the more mature roots can be used direct from the garden; and last and perhaps most important, carrots can be harvested and stored for winter use.

Carrots will do best in light soil, and it should be well and deeply prepared if you want to grow good ones. Stony, lumpy, hard soil will produce stunted and twisted roots. Carrots should be thinned properly as well, for adjacent roots are apt to twine themselves one about the other. The seeds are slow to germinate, and some recommend that a marker crop be sowed along with them as in the case of parsnips. I have never found this to be necessary. The seeds may be sown as early as the soil can be prepared, although it is best to wait until the ground is slightly warm. Sow them one-half inch deep, as thinly as possible in the row—say, thirty to forty seeds to a foot—and tamp and pat the soil down over them. The rows should be twelve inches apart.

When the plants are well started, they should be thinned to stand one and a half to two inches apart. This thinning can be postponed until the little carrots are the size of a slate-pencil up to lead-pencil size; and the thinnings, as stated, can be used as a salad garnish or as a relish. Carrots should carefully be kept free of weeds, particularly when they are small, as weeds will soon smother them completely if given a chance.

If the garden is located where there is a long growing season, it might be well to make two plantings of carrots, the first as early as possible for immediate use, the second a month later for autumn and winter use.

The varieties recommended are, for early use, the *Chantenay;* and the *Hutchingson,* a late heavy-yielding variety, for storage and winter use. The planting of these two varieties should, in most cases, eliminate the need for a second planting. One-fourth ounce of seeds of each variety should be more than sufficient to plant three fifty-foot rows.

The carrot has one definite claim upon the affection of the gardener—it presents no great problem in pest control. I have never had any trouble with either disease or insects; and I feel safe in stating that in a small subsistence garden attention will not have to be given to carrot pests or diseases.

SWISS CHARD

Swiss chard, which is actually a variety of the common beet, is granted a place in the garden because of its value as a long-season producer of good greens. Unlike spinach, which produces but one crop, the outer leaves of the chard can be snipped off with shears and the supply will be constantly renewed by growth from the center. The stalks or stems of the heavy outside leaves can be cooked like celery or asparagus, and are delicious.

Swiss chard will thrive throughout the summer, and will continue to produce long after the first frosts have come. The seeds should be scattered sparingly in rows twelve inches apart, and covered to the depth of about one-half inch. The well-started plants should be thinned to stand about five inches apart, and the thinnings can be used for greens. One-fourth ounce of seeds should be ample for planting one fifty-foot row. The variety recommended is *Fordhook Giant.*

Swiss chard has never presented me with any problem of pest or disease control. The Department of Agriculture warns of two enemies, one insect and one disease. The disease, commonly known as leaf-spot, can be controlled by severe cutting back of the leaves affected. The insect, the blister beetle, is best controlled by picking them off by hand. The beetle is long and slender, with a black, gray or striped body. Leaves damaged by the blister beetle should be discarded as unfit for use.

BEETS

Beets are another valuable member of the home-garden family, for they produce greens; tender young beets for immediate table use; roots for storage and winter use; and they are excellent both pickled and canned. They produce well, and are high in food value.

Beets may be planted as early in the spring as the soil can be worked. Inasmuch as they are apt to become woody in texture if left too long in the ground, it is well to make two plantings, the second one in midsummer for fall and winter use. In this case, one of the two rows allotted on the plan to beets can be planted to spinach, which will be cleaned out in time for the second planting of beets.

The seeds should be scattered sparingly, as each of the seedballs may contain more than one seed. The seeds of the first planting, in the moist soil of spring, need only be barely covered and then tamped or firmed over with the hand. The midsummer planting, if one is made, should be deeper; if the soil is dry, as deep as two inches, the earth then firmly tamped down over the row and raked over lightly with the garden rake. The rows should stand twelve inches apart, and the plants thinned to about three inches apart. The thinnings make excellent greens. One ounce of seeds should be ample to plant two fifty-foot rows, particularly if the seeds are sown sparingly, as they should be. The variety recommended is the *Detroit*, a high-quality beet for table, canning, or storage.

The enemies of the beet are the same as those of Swiss chard, although the control is different. Inasmuch as the tops are not eaten—except the thinnings—they can be sprayed for the control of leaf-spot. The recommended treatment involves using a spray containing two tablespoons of zineb per gallon of water when disease first appears. Repeat every seven days as long as moist weather prevails. Do not use zineb within seven days of harvest. The blister beetle can be controlled by hand, by knocking the bugs into a can of kerosene.

SUMMER SQUASH

Summer squash should not be left out of the subsistence garden, even though very little space is allotted to them. The squash is the most prodigious and phenomenal producer in terms of pounds that I know. I have made no detailed investigation nor have I kept accurate records, but rough computations indicate that one hill of summer squash, the combined roots of which certainly do not occupy more than one cubic foot of earth, will produce at least fifty pounds of fruit. This is one of the incomprehensible mysteries of nature.

Among the many summer squash—summer crookneck, straightneck, simlan, white bush scallop, zucchini, cocozelle—there is only one variety which I can whole-heartedly recommend, and that is the cocozelle. To my mind, it is far and away the most satisfactory summer squash to cultivate. It is a bush type plant, and thus does not take up much room; it is a prolific producer; and by common consent it is the most pleasant of all as an item of diet. The summer squash can be used over a long productive season as a fresh vegetable, and it can be successfully canned for winter use.

Winter squash are omitted from the garden plan because they require more room than their value warrants.

Squash prefer moist rich soil, and will do best if a shovelful of well-rotted manure is placed in every hill. The plan calls for but four hills of squash. These hills are four feet apart. Each hill should be excavated to the depth of six or eight inches, a generous shovelful of well-rotted manure placed in the bottom of the hole and mixed with topsoil, then a layer of topsoil at least one inch deep should cover the mixture of manure and earth. Six or seven seeds should be planted in each hill and covered to the depth of about one inch. They should not be planted until all danger of frost is past, for the leaves are very tender and susceptible to freezing. The fruits should be gathered and used as soon as they are large enough—in the case of cocozelle twelve to fourteen inches long—while the skin is still tender.

I have never had any trouble at all with pests or disease. Squash are subject to certain leaf-spot diseases, however, and if they should appear on leaves or stems, a Bordeaux mixture spray should be used.

CUCUMBERS

It is claimed that cucumbers have no great actual food value. They provide, however, a very important source of pickles and relishes, and even though it is wise to devote the main part of one's efforts to the producing of substantial vegetables, pickles and relishes definitely have their place in the winter menu. Cucumbers besides, eaten fresh from the garden, add variety and interest to salads.

The culture of cucumbers is very similar to that of summer squash. They, too, are very sensitive to frost and should not be planted until all danger of frost is past. Ten or a dozen seeds to a hill is sufficient, and the plants should be thinned to a half-dozen after they are well started.

The variety recommended, if only one variety is used, is the *Straight Eight,* an early symmetrical cucumber eight inches long, deep green when ready to use. A half-ounce packet of seeds is more than enough for the planting indicated on the plan.

The striped cucumber beetle is the only enemy which has attacked the cucumbers in my garden, and this insect can be controlled with Sevin. The plants are subject to a bacterial wilt. Control cucumber beetles that spread this disease. Begin shortly after seedlings emerge or transplants are put in field and continue on a seven-day schedule early in the season.

SPINACH

Spinach could be planted in twelve-inch rows, but several considerations make it seem wise to have the first planting between the rows of the high or telephone peas. Spinach likes the same kind of soil and moisture conditions that are favorable to peas; it can be planted early, as early as the peas, and the crop will be out of the way before the peas are far enough advanced to interfere in any way, for it can be picked within six weeks after planting. No thinning of the plants is necessary if the rather large seeds are scattered at about the rate of fifteen to a foot of row. The first pickings should be in the nature of a thinning, removing alternate plants, so that progressively the others are left farther and farther apart.

Spinach is one of the most important of all the garden vegetables. It supplies the first really good garden dish perhaps— and home-grown spinach is a very different vegetable from the spinach bought at the grocery-store. It is one of the most successful canned vegetables, coming from the jars in winter with all the succulence and flavor of freshly picked leaves. Successive plantings can be made so that the supply of spinach is practically continuous throughout the season in northern climates. The first row of early carrots to be pulled can be replanted to spinach. The space that the telephone peas make available after they are pulled can be planted to a later sowing.

To hasten germination the seeds should be soaked in water at room temperature for forty-eight hours before planting. The soil should be non-acid, finely prepared, and fertile. Side dressing of sodium nitrate should be made to promote vigorous leaf growth.

Popular varieties are the *Long Standing Bloomsdale* for spring planting and the *Virginia Savoy* for fall planting. The latter is resistant to yellows, or blight as is the *Hybrid No. 7*. It is well to purchase four ounces of each variety, early and late, so that there will be plenty of seeds for all the plantings that may be desired. This amount will leave a surplus of seeds, to be sure, but at the current price of ten cents for a four-ounce package, no great loss will be incurred if some seeds are left over. However, if the seeds can be purchased in two-ounce packets, one each of these would be sufficient.

Insect pests can be controlled by using Diazinon not later than 14 days prior to harvest. Diseases include downy mildew and blight. Mildew can be controlled by using a spray containing maneb. However, it is best to avoid the problem by using resistant varieties. Again, blight is controlled by the use of resistant varieties. These are, in addition to those already mentioned, *Dixie Market* and *Old Dominion*.

ENDIVE

Endive is a hardy plant grown for use as a salad. It excels as a late summer and fall salad green, and it is for this use that endive is included in the plan. It will withstand considerable frost, and it is the salad vegetable I have always used for transplanting to the cold frame to be available for winter greens.

The seeds should be planted one-half inch deep; and the plants should stand twelve inches apart, with twenty inches between rows. The recommended varieties are *Full Heart Batavian* and *Salad King*. A quarter-ounce package is the smallest amount available and is more than enough for the planting as indicated on the plan.

PEAS

It has not been until the last two seasons that I have had real success in growing peas. Perhaps the lack of great success, coupled with the fact that peas require a disproportionate amount of space for the amount of produce, has prejudiced me somewhat. While I readily admit that they are one of the finest fruits of the garden to eat, their place in the subsistence garden is not as truly important as is the lowly spinach, for instance.

First of all, peas will not do well in dry soil. Second, they are a cool-season crop. Third, they will not thrive if sown thickly. Fourth, the seeds should be planted deep enough—early peas two to four inches deep, and later ones two inches. If all these conditions are observed, and the seeds are planted in fertile, well-drained but not dry soil, a good crop should result provided that disease and insects are kept under control.

Early peas are of the dwarf or bush variety. Late peas are of the tall variety. One row of early peas, which is in reality a double row, is indicated on the plan. The seeds should be planted as early in the spring as the ground can be prepared. It is generally understood that it is not necessary to give any support to vines of the dwarf varieties; but in my experience, the trouble it takes to "brush" them lightly will be amply repaid.

If access to some brush lot can be had, two or three armfuls of twigs three feet long—easily cut with a good pair of garden snips—should be enough to brush a fifty-foot row. The twigs should be forced into the ground to the depth of four inches or so, and placed near enough together so that the branches overlap. This should be done after the soil is prepared for planting and before the seeds are sown. After the brush is in place a row can be sown on each side and three inches away from it.

The seeds should not be closer together than three inches; or, to insure a good stand, they can be planted more thickly and thinned to three inches apart after the plants have started. These seeds should be at least three inches deep, and the soil should be well firmed down over them after planting. In preparing the soil I used a commercial concentrated fertilizer which I scattered thinly in the bottom of the trench, and then mixed thoroughly with earth. Fertilizer should not be permitted to come in contact with the seeds.

The tall peas should be planted at approximately the same time as the bush peas; in any event before hot dry weather is imminent. Peas yield best if early sowings are made. In the case of tall peas, support must be provided for the vines. I have used five-foot-wide chicken wire, two-inch mesh, as a support for my tall, or telephone peas. This has proved perfectly satisfactory and it requires the minimum of trouble.

Two double rows are indicated on the plan, and for this

eight fairly stout stakes, two to three inches in diameter and seven feet long, are required. The stakes should be sharpened and driven two feet into the ground, one at each end of a row, and two in between, evenly spaced. The wire is then tacked to the stakes in such a manner that it can be easily removed from the posts, rolled up and stored for use another season. It is best to have the wire in place before the seeds are planted. A row

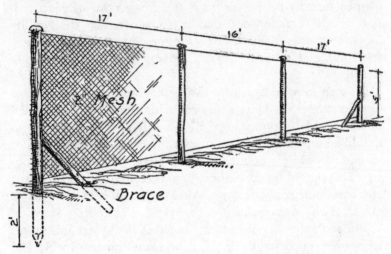

STAKING WIRE FOR TALL PEAS

Figure 10

may then be planted on each side of the wire, two inches deep, so the plants will be four inches apart rather than the three inches indicated for dwarf peas; also each row should be slightly farther away from the support than the distance indicated for dwarf peas.

Thomas Laxton, Greater Progress, Little Marvel, Freezonia and *Giant Stride* are recommended as suitable early varieties with wrinkled seeds. *Wando* has considerable heat resistance. *Alderman* and *Lincoln* are approximately two weeks later than *Greater Progress* but under favorable conditions yield heavily. *Alderman* is a desirable variety for growing on brush or a trellis. Peas grown on supports are less liable to destruction by birds.

There can be no doubt about the best tall late pea for the home garden. It is the *Alderman* (Telephone) pea. This pea produces more per vine than do the early peas, and it bears over a long picking season. It takes seventy-two days to reach maturity. It is also a wilt-resistant variety. One pound of seeds of the dwarf variety should suffice, and two pounds of the telephone peas.

The enemies of peas unfortunately are several. I have had less trouble with early peas than with the late ones. The diseases listed by different authorities seem not to have been the kind which attacked my peas. Therefore, in enumerating them, my information is at best secondhand. Diseases include fusarium wilt, root rots and virus diseases. If wilt is a problem, use resistant varieties and plant in soil not containing the fungus. For rots, avoid soil previously planted in pea. Virus diseases, again, are best avoided by using resistant varieties.

The pea aphid is an insect that attacks the plants and stunts their growth. It is best controlled before they become too numerous beneath the leaves. Use Diazinon or malathion for this purpose. It should also be noted that the aphids spread virus diseases so that controlling them will help to prevent the spread of the diseases. In a small garden these insects may not be too much of a problem but plants should be examined carefully in case they should appear.

BEANS

Six different varieties of beans are listed on the plan. Of these there are two varieties of shell beans, two varieties of snapbeans, and two varieties of limabeans. The plan shows one row of bush limas and one row of pole limas (optional). I have not raised pole limas in my garden, for the growing season is too short to get a crop. They are a more satisfactory crop than the bush limas, however, so they are included in the list.

Of the snapbeans, or stringbeans, one is a pole bean and one is a bush bean. Both of the shell beans are for a dried crop to be stored and used in winter; or they are excellent canned, the red kidney bean in particular. Snapbeans are used green, pods and all. Shell beans are allowed to mature on the vine and the dried beans are shelled out of the hard pods. Limabeans are shelled and used green.

Beans of all varieties are susceptible to frost. None of them should be planted, therefore, until all danger of frost is past and the soil is warm. The soil should be well drained, well supplied with humus, and moderately rich. Beans, in common with other legumes, have the ability to extract nitrogen from the air and are therefore soil builders rather than soil depleters.

The seeds should not be planted too deep; if the soil is moist, one to two inches is sufficient; if the soil is dry, plant them deeper, and firm the earth well over them. Beans may be soaked before planting to insure more rapid sprouting. Some beans are planted in hills, others in rows; in no case should they be closer together than three to four inches. I have used a concentrated commercial fertilizer (Vigoro) sparingly in the hills and rows, well mixed with earth and covered so that the seeds do not come in direct contact with the fertilizer. One thing is important whatever the variety—beans must not be cultivated while the leaves are wet. Touching the wet plants spreads the spores of anthracnose, or bean canker, from the soil to the plant and from one plant to another.

Snapbeans, or Stringbeans: The bush stringbean recommended is the bush waxbean. They may be planted in either hills or rows. Having tried both, I prefer the row. The seeds should not be planted more than one inch deep if the soil is moist, and not closer together than four inches, and they must not come in contact with any fertilizer. A half-pound of seeds should be sufficient. A recommended variety is the *Kinghorn Wax. Tendercrop, Topcrop, Contender,* and *Harvester* are also good types.

The pole stringbean, or snapbean, as the name indicates, is a tall vine which requires the support of a pole. The poles should be eight or nine feet tall, set well in the ground, and three feet apart each way. The seeds should be planted an inch and a half deep, five or six seeds to a hill. The variety recommended is the *Kentucky Wonder*, a very prolific and delicious stringbean, which is equally good fresh or canned. It may also be used as a dry bean. The amount indicated on the plan will produce more than can possibly be used on the table, and will provide an ample surplus for canning; or part of the surplus may be left on the vines and harvested as shell beans for winter use. One-half pound of seeds should be sufficient for the two rows indicated.

Shell Beans: Of the shell beans recommended, the red kidney is a prime winter bean, good dried, but particularly good canned. The seeds may be planted just after the very last frosts of spring when the soil is slightly warm, for the plants are especially sensitive to cold and frost. But they are easy to grow, and if the soil conditions are right it is not difficult to get a good stand. The seeds should be planted one inch deep, if the soil is moist; slightly deeper if the soil is dry; and they should not come in contact with fertilizer. A half-pound is generally the minimum package and will provide sufficient seeds for one fifty-foot row.

Even better is the other shell bean, *French's Horticultural*, with a flavor surpassing that of the red kidney, and excellent dried for winter use. This variety requires the same handling as does the kidney bean, the same amount of seeds, the same soil conditions. When the pods are still green the beans are delicate in flavor, and can be used fresh from the garden as limabeans are used; and they are much easier to grow to maturity than limabeans.

Limabeans: Of the limabeans only the quickest maturing bush limas can be grown in my climate. As a matter of fact, I have had but two successful seasons out of three growing them, and as far as I know my garden has produced the only limas in this neighborhood. The Fordhook, a bush lima, requires seventy-five days to mature. The pole limas require eighty-five days.

The plan devotes two rows to limabeans and, if conditions justify it, one row may be devoted to each variety. The pole lima bears more prolifically than does the bush. Planting instructions for bush limas are the same as those for the other bush beans; and for pole limas the directions for the *Kentucky Wonder* may be followed. Of the many varieties, the *Fordhook* bush lima and the *King of the Garden* pole lima are well recommended.

Insect pests include seed corn maggots, aphids, Mexican bean beetles, and spider mites. Maggots are controlled by treating seeds prior to planting. Some seed is treated with insecticide when purchased and is so indicated on the package. If not, treat as follows: mix ¼ teaspoon of 75% dieldrin wettable powder with every four pounds of seed by shaking in a paper bag or glass jar. For smaller lots of seed, use correspondingly less insecticide. Be sure to wear gloves when handling seed. Use a malathion spray for aphids before they become numerous beneath the leaves in summer. Malathion or Sevin can be used against the Mexican bean beetle, and Kelthane is used for spider mites, again, before they become numerous beneath the leaves in summer.

Diseases are leaf spots, rust, and mosaic viruses. Leaf spots are dead and dying spots on leaves. Plant western-grown seed. No seed treatment is effective in controlling this disease. Rust is indicated by powdery red or black pustules on leaves. Spray with two tablespoons of maneb or zineb per gallon of water, beginning when disease is first observed on leaves and continuing every ten days until harvest. Do not use maneb within four days or zineb within seven days of harvest.

Finally, mosaic viruses are indicated by mottled light and dark green areas on the leaves. Plant resistant varieties and control aphids since they spread the viruses.

CABBAGE

The plan allows for two plantings of cabbage—one of early cabbage in a row of its own; the other, the late cabbage, to be planted after the bush peas are pulled and in the space the peas occupied.

Cabbage is a very important, however plebeian, member of the select group of vegetables indicated for the garden. Served green as salad and cole-slaw, fresh and crisp from the garden, it is delicious. It is an important cooked vegetable, boiled or creamed; and with very little trouble it can be turned into sauerkraut and kept for winter use. More than that, cabbage can also be stored for winter use, and it is thus that it is most valuable perhaps, for it gives the family table a green vegetable at a time when it is most welcome. Greens are necessary for a properly balanced diet, and the cabbages in the summer garden supply the family with homely but healthful greens even in the depth of winter.

Cabbages are young plants, called "sets," when they are placed in the garden row. These sets can either be raised from seeds by the gardener, or purchased. I always buy my sets, knowing that the trained hand of the professional greenhouse man can produce better sets than I can raise. Plants for the early varieties must be grown under cover, while those for the late varieties can be grown outdoors.

The gardener can either purchase his seeds and have his plants grown to order by a local greenhouse, in which case he can select the variety he chooses; or he can purchase the sets direct from the grower, being limited in this case to the variety, both early and late, which is available.

Cabbages require rich moist soil, and if you can provide this and protect them from their enemies, you will be richly rewarded for the small amount of cash and labor invested.

The early plants may be set out as soon as the soil is prepared and the danger of a hard frost is past. They should be placed twelve inches apart; and when they are set it is wise to "puddle" them. The hole to receive the plant can be made with a pointed stick and filled with water before the plant is set. After the plant is dropped into the hole, the roots well down, the soil should be firmly pressed about the lower stem so that no air-pocket remains around the roots. The use of nitrate as a side dressing is recommended to promote vigorous growth. Four dozen plants have been indicated on the plan.

Late cabbage seeds can be planted in a small prepared seed-bed out of doors in one corner of the garden. The soil should be only moderately fertile, to insure a good growth of roots. The seeds should be sown in rows six inches apart and thinly, so that the sets can be transplanted directly from the seed-bed to the garden. They need not be set out before the first of July, and should be placed eighteen inches apart.

The procedure in the handling of both late and early cabbage will vary, depending on the length of the growing season. In my Vermont climate I do not make two plantings of cabbage. I set all plants out at the same time, the early cabbage maturing for summer use, and the late, slower-growing varieties maturing for fall and winter use. There can be no absolute rule given, for conditions vary greatly in different localities. If the climate is such that a simultaneous planting of both early and late cabbage seems advisable, then a half-row—two dozen plants—can be set out in the row reserved for cauliflower, limiting the cauliflower to only two dozen plants; and the row indicated on the plan for early cabbage can be set to four dozen late cabbage plants. Remember that late cabbage should not be set out too early. The heads will mature in warm weather and burst and so be lost, unless they are immediately converted into sauerkraut.

The recommended early varieties are: Of the Copenhagen type, the *Golden Acre,* maturing in seventy days and of the Wakefield type, the *Jersey Wakefield.* The *Danish Ballhead* is an excellent late, round cabbage. Where cabbage yellows is a serious problem, resistant varieties should be used, including *Wisconsin Hollander,* for late storage; *Wisconsin All Seasons,* a kraut cabbage, somewhat earlier; *Marion Market* and *Globe,* round-head cabbages, for midseason.

Three enemies of the cabbage have bothered my garden: club-root, cabbage worms, and maggots. Club-root is caused by a slime mold. It is first noticed when the young plants wilt and droop. If one of these affected plants is pulled it will be seen that the roots are enlarged and distorted, with great swollen masses on them which soon decay and stink. The disease will kill some plants, but even the ones which manage to survive will never amount to anything. The disease is in the soil and the spores of the slimy mold will live there for at least seven years.

Various controls are suggested by different authorities. After having had several seasons when nearly every plant in my garden was affected, I have had no sign of club-root on my cabbages or any of the other crucifers since I applied wood ashes as a control for the onion maggot. I give this for what it is worth. I have not had sufficient time to collect data which will provide convincing proof that wood ashes will control club-root. As far as I know, no other factors have entered the problem, so it would seem reasonably sure that the cause of the disappearance of club-root from my cabbage was the application of wood ashes. At least no harm will result from trying, for the ashes will not burn cabbages; on the contrary, they feed them and promote their growth.

Methods of control suggested by the authorities are: Select seedbed in area where cabbage was not previously grown. Do not transplant into field where previous crop was affected.

The maggot can be controlled by the use of wood ashes, as in the case of onions.

The cabbage worm can be combated by killing the white butterflies which lay the eggs that produce the worms, or by smashing the yellow egg-clusters which appear underneath the leaves of the cabbage, or by picking off the worms when they appear. These green worms, about one and a quarter inches long, also can be controlled by the use of Sevin or Thiodan sprays, applied once per week under the leaf surface.

CAULIFLOWER

A row of cauliflower has been indicated in the garden plan— or a half-row if the alternate cabbage planting is used as suggested, or a half-row of broccoli. Cauliflower is generally rated as being difficult to grow; but it so delicious as a vegetable, and there are so many other uses for it, picked fresh in the home garden, that it has been included, if only for a trial. It is always welcome as a table vegetable, and it is also valuable as a pickle.

Being a very close relative of cabbage, the general discussion of cabbage applies to the cauliflower as well. I suggest the purchase of the young plants from a greenhouse—two dozen for a half-row, four dozen for a full row. The plants require moist soil and will not thrive in dry. They require rich soil with plenty of available plant food. I have had uniformly good success with cauliflower, and attribute this success to the fact that the soil is moist and rich, and that our Vermont summers are never extremely dry. I have always used, and recommend, side dressings of nitrate through the growing season.

When the cauliflower heads begin to form, the outer leaves should be drawn up and over the heads and tied in a bunch with a bit of string. This protects them from the sun and rain and insures solid white heads.

All the diseases and pests of the cabbage are also enemies of the cauliflower and the controls are the same.

Other members of this family which are desirable in the vegetable garden, such as kale and brussels-sprouts, have been omitted from the plan. Broccoli is a prolific producer and is a much more certain crop than cauliflower, and it can be substituted for cauliflower if the taste of the family or the lack of success with cauliflower should make this seem wise. While brussels-sprouts will yield long after the hard frosts come, they do not yield in proportion to the other crucifers. For this reason they are omitted because of lack of space.

TOMATOES

In the family subsistence garden each vegetable must pay its own way. Tomatoes are the one vegetable which can be canned by a factory just as well as at home, and more cheaply; it does not pay the home canner to bother with them. They cannot be stored for winter as can many other vegetables. Therefore they must be used as they mature.

Six healthy and vigorous tomato plants will supply the average family with all the tomatoes they will want to eat fresh from the garden. I realize that this is heresy and have recanted to the extent of including one whole row of tomatoes in the plan. This allows for seventeen plants set three feet apart. If the plants are healthy and fruitful, they will produce more tomatoes than are actually needed, unless some of them are canned.

There is an infinite variety of tomatoes to choose from, starting with the tiny currant-tomato up to the mammoth kinds which produce fruits weighing as much as a pound apiece. There are four colors: purple, scarlet, orange and yellow; and there is a whole sliding-scale of tastes from the acid to the sweet.

The plants can be home-raised from seeds started in the house, in flats or cans; but they can more easily be purchased at the store or greenhouse. Stocky, deep-green plants should be selected. And they should not be set out in the garden until after all danger of frost is past. For fertilizer, wood ashes are to be preferred to manure or nitrogen-bearing fertilizers, as the latter tend to grow plants which are more stem and leaves than fruit.

As the tomato plants develop they should be staked and tied with strips of old rag. It has been proved that pruning or pinching back the vines does not produce more or finer fruit, and that this procedure is a waste of time.

The only enemy of the tomato with which I have had experience is the leaf-hopper, which can be controlled with a Sevin spray. A large green worm, called the hornworm, also thrives on tomato plants. It can be controlled by hand-picking into a can of kerosene.

Leaf-spot, a fungus disease, causes light circular spots with dark margins to appear on the leaves, starting on the lower leaves and working up, causing them to drop off as the disease progresses upward. Spraying with a maneb solution will control this.

The tomato wilt is another disease caused by a fungus, and if it appears in the home garden, wilt-resistant species, such as *Porte, Enterpriser* and *Fireball,* should be planted.

SWEET CORN

The vegetable to which the plan devotes more garden space than any other comes last. Corn takes up a great deal of space in proportion to the amount of harvest received. In pounds, at any rate, corn cannot be compared with summer squash. If there were such a thing as a national vegetable—as there is a national bird, for instance—sweet corn would surely be it. In the face of such popularity, I am afraid that any reasons I might advance in favor of devoting more space to other, more productive and less soil-depleting vegetables would be harshly received. In a garden of this size there is room for corn. If the garden space must be less than the plan indicates, then I urge that corn be the first vegetable to be eliminated.

Sweet corn cannot stand frost, and therefore should not be planted until all danger of frost is over and the soil is warm. Corn will not do well in wet, heavy, poorly drained soil; the soil should be rich and above all well drained. The hills should stand two feet apart each way; and in each hill there should be placed a small spadeful of well-rotted manure, covered with soil before the seeds are dropped; the seeds are then covered and firmed down. Four stalks to the hill are plenty; but recalling the old jingle,

> One for the cutworm, one for the crow,
> One for the blackbird, and three for to grow,

perhaps it is wise to drop six seeds in each hill and then thin to three or four stalks after the plants are started.

In some places more than one planting of corn may be desirable, but ordinarily one planting of three different varieties, each with a different maturing date, is better. Because corn depends upon wind-blown pollination to produce the ears, it should always be planted in a group of several rows rather than one long row. Do not remove the suckers or shoots which spring out from the stalk at the ground, for they help to nourish the plant.

A pound and a half of seeds should be sufficient to plant the ten rows on the plan; if three varieties are grown, one-half pound of each; or two varieties, three-quarters of a pound each. Bear in mind that these are not hard-and-fast rules for the selection of varieties or the amounts to be planted, but merely a suggested guide.

There are two standard varieties of sweet corn. *Golden Bantam* is an early variety, requiring about ninety days to mature. *Stowell's Evergreen,* a late variety, requires one hundred and seven days to reach maturity. These are the varieties I recommend for cultivation where the growing season will permit of the maturing of the *Evergreen.* If the season is shorter, I should use *Gold Cup,* which matures in eighty-two days, and *Golden Bantam,* which comes along about ten days later. A good combination is three rows each of *Gold Cup* and *Golden Bantam,* and four rows of *Country Gentleman* or *Stowell's Evergreen.*

The enemies of the corn which have come to plague my garden are very few indeed. Very rarely a corn smut; one year a very few (possibly three or four affected ears) corn-borers, and again two years later one or two ears affected by the corn-borer; that is all. Bacterial wilt is another disease that attacks corn, causing yellow streaking of the leaves and stunted plants. Insecticides should be used to control the flea beetles that spread the disease. Wilt-resistant varieties should also be used.

Other insect pests are the seed corn maggot, flea beetle, corn earworm, and aphids. Maggots are best controlled by treating seeds prior to planting. A Sevin spray can be used on earworms, which first appear usually in early July. Aphids are controlled by using a malathion spray.

This concludes the list of vegetables which are given on the garden plan. Fuller details as to fertilizers, sprays and dusts will be found in the Appendix. As stated previously, this list is purely tentative and can be changed to suit the tastes and preferences of each individual gardener. In fact, in any garden, the list will probably be changed from year to year.

It will be noted on the plan that the last fifteen feet of the garden is devoted to peas, early and late; and that late cabbage is to go in after the early pea vines are pulled. This whole space can then include whatever the taste of the gardener indicates for second plantings. The late cabbage can be alternated with lettuce heads. One or two rows of late spinach can be planted and there will still be room for another row of radishes, another row each of late beets and late carrots, and another row of Swiss chard.

This gives the gardener a wide latitude in adjusting the second plantings to his own particular tastes or needs.

CHAPTER IV

THE CARE OF THE GARDEN

GOOD SEED, sound planning, and careful planting, coupled with favorable weather and well-prepared soil, and the garden is off to a flying start. From this point on, its success or failure depends upon the care and skill with which the gardener performs his main task. This task is the cultivation and protection of the growing plants. Frost or flood or drought may circumvent him, it is true, but for the most part a determined gardener can bring his garden through a successful harvest despite hail and high water.

The task of growing the garden is twofold. First, to cultivate the plants, giving them the ideal conditions under which to grow; and second, to protect them from their many enemies.

Perhaps the greatest task of cultivation is the control of weeds; but that is not all. In addition to weed control, cultivation includes tillage, which aerates the soil, breaks the crust, and forms a dust mulch which prevents the evaporation of moisture from the soil. It includes the feeding of the plants, if this is advisable, and the watering of the plants as well. Thinning the plants in the row, so that each may have the proper space in which to develop, is also a part of cultivation.

The tillage of the soil should start as soon as the seed sprouts break the surface of the ground enough to make the row visible. The first cultivation is extremely important, for it gives the seedlings the head-start which they must have if they are to overcome the weeds. It is much less labor to keep the weeds down than it is to get them down; and in the matter of weed control this first cultivation is the most important of all. It should be as close to the row as may be made without disturbing the growing plants, and should be deep.

The second cultivation should be done following the first rain after the first cultivation, but in no case more than one week later. By this time most vegetables will be grown enough so that it is possible to weed close to each plant, and thus to eliminate all weeds in the row. Between-row cultivation should keep weeds down between the rows, but most vegetables require at least one going over by hand to remove the weeds from around the plants. By the time the third cultivation takes place, the plants should be well enough grown so that they are dominant, and weeds in the rows should present no great problem.

Weeds are the main cause of garden failure. They rob the garden plants of food and sunlight, and they are hosts to insects and diseases. Of the three kinds of weeds, annuals, biennials and perennials, the annuals are the most numerous and the most bothersome to the gardener. One perennial, however, causes an undue amount of trouble. This is witch-grass, or quack-grass as it is sometimes called. It is usually the worst problem the gardener has, at least in the New England and nearby States.

As the annuals seed and die in one season, their prosperity can be considerably checked if by careful watch they are never allowed to go to seed. Seeds of annuals, however, will find their way into the garden in spite of all precautions, and barnyard manure is one of the worst offenders. Fortunately, most of their young stalks are tender and their roots shallow, and early and continued cultivation between the rows of vegetables, and at least one good row weeding, should keep them under control. It is always easier to keep them under control from the beginning than it is to get them under control once they have a good start. There are no annual weeds in the vegetable garden which cannot easily be controlled by weeding and cultivation.

The witch-grass requires an entirely different technique. If you have no witch-grass in your garden, you may consider yourself lucky. However, witch-grass seems to be a sure indication of a good garden spot; it prefers rich, well-drained, moist soil, and if there is witch-grass around, you may be sure you will find it in your garden if your garden is in the ideal spot. The presence of witch-grass, indeed, might be used as an indication of the best place to choose for a vegetable garden. It is such a strong, resourceful, and insidious enemy, however, that many old hands will choose a less favorable location for their garden rather than take on a battle with witch-grass. But this is laziness or cowardice; witch-grass can be whipped.

It is a tough grass, with a broad leaf, somewhat like the leaf of timothy grass, and it grows a head which resembles that of grain—wheat or rye. The characteristic which makes it so hard to combat in the garden is its so-called root system. The long, sharp-pointed roots—which are not actually roots but underground stems—grow deep and horizontally, sending numerous shoots up to the surface. The points of these roots, as they are generally called, are spearlike, and will readily grow right through a potato, but the root itself is quite tender, so that when pulled to remove it from the soil it breaks—and therein lies the secret of the success of witch-grass. Each bit of underground stem remaining in the soil, however small it may be, if it has a joint in it, will grow and start a whole new series of shoots and roots. Even bits left carelessly on the ground will soon become tufts of witch-grass.

The only way to get rid of it is to watch for every green shoot that pokes up through the soil, then with a potato-hook dig deep, follow back along each underground stem, and remove every one of them. Carry them away from the garden entirely, stack them up to dry, and burn them. Plowing and harrowing in the spring only tends to spread the grass, for the prolific underground stems are broken up and scattered.

Repeated harrowing in dry weather will discourage it, and pigs will root it out and eventually kill it; but as neither of these methods seems suitable for the home garden, I advise you to search it out and grub it out by the hand method. My own garden, which is completely surrounded by a magnificent stand of witch-grass, is kept free of it by this method with no great amount of trouble.

The technique of weed control and cultivation are the next

considerations. The garden plot indicates that the rows of small stuff are twelve inches apart. This is for two reasons. One is to conserve space, and the other is to help in the control of weeds. Weeds will not thrive in the shade. If the battle for sunlight waged between weeds and vegetables receives no help or hindrance from the gardener, the most vigorous, fastest-growing plants will win. But if the weed competition is removed, the vegetables will have that much more strength to put into the growing of luxuriant foliage and plentiful fruits.

Thus it can be seen that if garden vegetables are to produce the maximum of growth they must be protected from weed competition for sunlight and food. Cultivating the vegetables and removing the weeds as soon as it is possible to do so enables the vegetables to gain the dominance, and this will make the gardener's task easier in combating later weeds.

There are two tools which I have found best for the cultivation of vegetable rows which are twelve inches apart. The first is the ordinary potato-hook, which may be purchased at any hardware store. The price varies from a dollar to a dollar and a half. The potato-hook has four long tines, each about eight inches long and curved, and the tines are about two inches apart. This tool is ideal for the first cultivation, for it permits of deep cultivation. The ground should be worked to the depth of three or four inches, and as close to the row as possible. This is best achieved by working backward, straddling the plants, and using alternate strokes of the hook on each side of the row.

The other tool is a steel garden rake, ten inches wide. After the rows are run through with the potato-hook (and this can be done rapidly), a second cultivation with the rake should follow. This breaks up any lumps that are left, smoothes the soil, and makes a finer mulch for retaining moisture.

The same procedure should be followed for all subsequent cultivation, and the cultivations should continue until the growth of the vegetables shades the rows sufficiently to make further tillage unnecessary. Onions, however, require cultivation until they are harvested, because of the fact that they afford no shade whatsoever.

In the later cultivations the second going-over with the rake is more important than in the earlier ones, for the potato-hook, while it does an excellent job of working the soil, merely up-roots the weeds. It does not cut them off as a hoe would; and so it is necessary to follow-up with the rake in order to remove the uprooted weeds from the soil. If left in place, particularly if a rain should follow the cultivation, many of them will take root again and continue to grow. Purslane—known to the

OGDENS HOE
place in vise, the mark
to be cut flush with jaws.
Score along jaws, with
sharp cold chisel, then
break with hammer.

Figure 11

farmer as pulsely or pussly—is one weed which will pick up and grow again under almost any conditions if it is not re-moved. The weeds thus raked up should be gathered and placed on the compost pile.

Until the growth of the plants makes further cultivation unnecessary, every part of the garden should be gone over at least once in every ten days. There can be no hard-and-fast rule for this, however, for the weather is an important factor. The soil should be worked after every rain, just as soon as its condition permits. It cannot be done satisfactorily while the soil is too wet, but should be done before it is thoroughly dry. Also, weeds will jump ahead after a rain, and it is well to get them before they get started. The garden should never be worked, however, while the plants are wet. As previously explained, this is particularly dangerous for beans; and the spores of fungus diseases may be picked up and spread to other plants as well.

After the first cultivation, subsequent workings should be shallower. As the roots develop, deep cultivation may injure them and thus slow the growth of the plants.

Wheel-hoes of different types are highly recommended for the cultivation of gardens. Their use is so widespread that they must have their good points. But the method I have described is the one that I find most satisfactory. It may be that others will find the use of the wheel-hoe quicker and easier. I prefer the potato-hook and the rake.

The garden hoe is another indispensable tool. There will be times when it will be necessary to cut weeds off below the surface of the ground, particularly if the weeds have achieved any considerable growth. Also, in cultivating corn and tomatoes the hoe can be used to good advantage. If the hoe is used to cultivate close to the rows and between the plants, a good idea is to cut the blade with a cold-chisel, diagonally from the neck to the bottom corner on each side, making the blade a sharp-pointed triangle as shown in the cut. This facilitates working in between close-growing plants.

Other tools the gardener will require are a flat-tined spading-fork, a wheelbarrow, another steel rake, sixteen inches across, a light crowbar, and a round-pointed shovel.

The fork is indispensable in spading the garden, and can also be used to handle manure. The wheelbarrow performs a multitude of services, from the handling of manure and material for the compost pile to the harvesting of the crops. The wide steel rake is necessary in preparing the soil for planting, as it covers more ground than the narrow one, and it also can be used for cultivating where the wider rows permit. The crowbar is invaluable in setting bean poles, staking tomatoes and peas, and if the soil is stony it will be a great help in removing the larger stones. The round-pointed shovel will find a hundred odd uses, from the preparing of hills for the planting of squash to the digging of drainage trenches.

Almost as damaging as weeds is too thick a growth of vegetables in the row; hence the importance of thinning. This should be done as soon as possible. Onions and carrots may be allowed to grow somewhat before thinning, and the thinnings can be used as salads. Beet and turnip thinnings can be used as greens.

After the plants in the garden are well started it often pays to feed them a little extra in order to get the best growth pos-

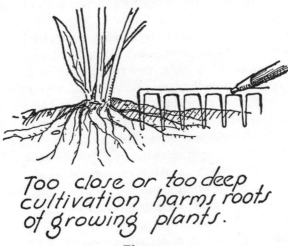

Too close or too deep
cultivation harms roots
of growing plants.

Figure 12

sible. Some fertilizers, nitrate in particular, are so soluble that if they were worked into the soil before planting they would leach away before the plants had a chance to make use of them. Therefore it is best that nitrates be applied after the plants have started their growth. Sodium nitrate is the form in which soluble nitrates can be made available to growing plants. Sodium nitrate is a white granular salt, which can be bought at the hardware or garden supply store. A ten-pound bag should be sufficient for the plot laid out.

Care should be exercised in applying sodium nitrate so that it does not touch the leaves or stem or roots of the plants which are being fed. It should be sprinkled on the soil alongside of the row, about two inches away from the plants. The granular salt can be allowed to trickle through the fingers as one walks along the row, stooped over with the hand fairly close to the ground. One handful should be sufficient to cover four or five feet. It is better to make several light applications than one heavy one.

As a general rule, nitrate should be fed only to plants of which neither the roots nor the fruit are to be used, for it promotes leaf growth at the expense of root growth and fruit. I have used side dressings of sodium nitrate with great success on cabbage, celery, spinach and lettuce.

There are several highly concentrated commercial fertilizers which can be used as side dressings. Some are applied as solids and some as liquids. As these concentrates are complete plant foods, they make excellent side dressing for vegetables whose growth is stunted or poor due to an insufficiency of plant food.

Root crops—beets, turnips and carrots—are generally helped by a side dressing of wood ashes. This is true also of onions.

Another form of side dressing is liquid manure. Liquid manure can be made by soaking manure in water. This and other liquid side dressings should be applied only while the soil is moist and should never come into direct contact with the plants.

Vegetables, in order to grow, require water as well as food and air and sunlight. Normally the rainfall of an area is sufficient to maintain the vegetation which it supports. Occasionally there will be a long period without rainfall, and then all vegetation suffers. It is part of the gardener's task to carry on in nature's place when she fails to provide the needed rain. In some areas there is a normal lack of rainfall sufficient to support vegetation other than cacti and their like, and irrigation is necessary to grow crops. However, in the ordinary garden a prolonged drought is the exception rather than the rule. Yet there remains a constant need for the gardener to maintain the moisture content of his garden soil.

Ordinarily this is done by cultivation. If the surface of the soil is kept in the proper condition, needless loss of moisture is prevented. Proper cultivation makes for the retention of moisture in the soil; improper cultivation may hasten its dissipation.

Heavy clay soils should not be worked while the soil is still wet. Clay is not only sticky and gluey when wet, but it tends to puddle and run together, baking into hard bricklike clods when the sun dries it. This lumpy surface condition is condu-

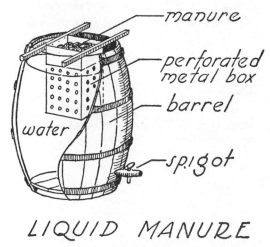

LIQUID MANURE

Figure 13

cive to rapid evaporation of moisture from the soil. On the other hand, clay soils, if cultivated or worked after the wet look or watery glisten has disappeared, will have as a result a finely broken-up surface. This loose pulverized earth on the ground forms a protective layer, or a "dust mulch," which keeps the soil from baking and drying out. This dust mulch is extremely important in the vegetable garden, for it serves as a protecting blanket which keeps the moisture in, and it prevents the rapid run-off of surface water when the rain falls.

If extreme dryness makes it necessary to use artificial watering, great care must be exercised. In all the several years that my vegetable garden has been in operation I have never watered any plant even once. This I believe is what the average gardener may expect. In normally moist climates the watering of the vegetable garden should never be necessary. But if your garden is in a dryer climate and the vegetables really need water, bear in mind a few well-established time-honored rules; for great harm can result from the improper application of water to the garden.

The first rule to be observed is: Do not water the garden until it really needs it, and then soak it. Occasional soakings are more important than frequent sprinklings. In fact, except for a few shallow-rooted plants, sprinklings will result in actual

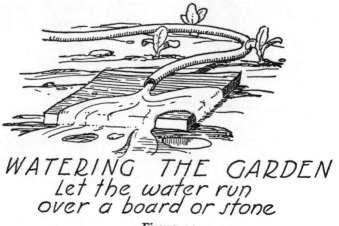

WATERING THE GARDEN
Let the water run
over a board or stone

Figure 14

harm; for the roots, in their search for this water, will become concentrated near the surface instead of penetrating deep, and when the sprinkling is omitted or a scorching sun beats down, the roots will be baked and the plants damaged.

When the ground is soaked, it should be done so that the earth is not washed away. If the water is run from a hose, the discharge should be directed onto a flat stone or a board, so that the flow of water is spread out and no one spot washed.

Light sandy loams require a great deal of water, but heavy clay soils must be watered more sparingly, for if they become water-soaked and soggy they are likely to turn sour.

The best time to water the garden is in the evening after the sun has gone down. The water will thus be able to sink in and penetrate before the sun gets a chance to evaporate it.

More of a hazard to the gardener than drought is unseasonable frost. In many parts of the country summer frosts or freezes are unheard-of, but in more than half of the United States unseasonable frosts are a reality, and when they come they can wreak havoc with a garden.

In planting the garden the expected normal frosts may be taken into account. The unseasonable frosts, on the other hand, have the gardener more or less at their mercy. Here are a few of the things that may be done to circumvent the summer freeze:

If there is any choice in the site of the garden, a location may be selected where the danger from freezing is lessened by the topography of the land. Cold air is heavier than warm and thus collects in the hollows and low places, which will be first to experience a summer freeze. A large body of water will act as a temperature adjuster; the water remains warm after the sun goes down, and thus warms the surrounding air. It also gives off mist or fog which acts as a protection against frost. The two points to remember, then, in choosing a site, if a choice is possible, are air drainage and the equalizing effects of a lake or other large body of water.

If after a storm the air clears with a north or northwest wind, and then at evening the wind falls, watch the thermometer. If the temperature is as low as forty degrees at sunset, frost may reasonably be expected. Fog, cloudy skies, and wind are dependable signs that frost will not occur; clear still nights are dangerous.

If all indications point to a frost, do what you can to minimize the damage. There is no blow more discouraging to the gardener than to survey the garden in the warm sunlight of the morning after a freeze. The squash leaves are black and drooping, the corn a deeper green and watery-looking, the beans all folded over, the cucumbers flat. Many varieties are not harmed by a moderate frost, so there is never a total loss, but nevertheless the loss sustained in one brief night after all the weeks of care and labor is a hard thing to have to bear.

When it is possible to forecast a summer freeze, two things can be done. Either cover the plants which are most susceptible to frost, or light fires or smudges in the garden. I have never tried fires or smudges, so have no first-hand knowledge as to their effectiveness. In a small garden it is possible to save all tender plants by covering them up. The vegetables shown on the plan which are tender and must be covered are squash, corn, tomatoes, cucumbers and all varieties of beans.

As these vegetables occupy nearly half of the entire garden—nineteen fifty-foot rows, to be exact—it is apparent that it will be quite a job to get everything covered. The squash and cucumbers do not present much of a problem. Dishcloths, towels, newspapers, almost anything in fact, can be used for covering them; even the slightest protection will ordinarily prevent damage from summer frost. The beans and corn present a real problem, the pole beans in particular. The best you can do is to cover as much as you can with whatever comes to hand, from sheets to newspapers, from boxes and cartons to straw or hay.

After the growing season is over, and frosts may be expected in due course, several expedients may be employed to prolong the usefulness of the garden in serving the table with fresh vegetables. Tomatoes which have not ripened on the vine and which are due to get caught by frost, may be picked green and ripened on a shelf set in a sunny window indoors. Green tomatoes can be kept a long while indoors, and are delicious served on the table if properly prepared. (A recipe is given in Chapter VI.)

If the garden boasts a cold frame, it may be put to excellent use at this time of the year. Lettuce and endive may be removed from the garden, with plenty of dirt about their roots, and heeled-in in the cold frame, and thus be available for use long after snow falls. Onions also may be transplanted to the cold frame if they have not matured by the time real frosts come. Salsify and parsnips may be left in the ground all winter, and may be used from the garden as late or as early as they can be dug. Ears of corn will ripen on stalks which have been killed by frost. Swiss chard, if protected by straw, will produce for the table long after the hard frosts come.

Worse than the vagaries of the weather, however, are the ravages of insects and disease. Drought and flood and frost are largely beyond the control of man, but they are not the gardener's common lot. On the other hand, insects of one kind or another, and disease in one form or another, are his daily concern. And in my own experience of the two, the bugs give the most trouble. Balance in nature is a wonderful thing. In stating that your tabby or tommy cat may have a very important bearing on the bugs in your garden I am tempted to tell the story of the upper New York State farmer who found his duck-shooting gradually disappearing. This story, told by one of the Conservation technicians of New York State, is a true one.

This farmer had on his farm a small pond which afforded excellent food and cover for ducks, and they regularly came in there on their fall flight south. The farmer enjoyed good shooting on his pond for years, then gradually the flights became fewer and fewer, and finally disappeared entirely. No more did ducks wheel and drop from autumn skies as they made their way south.

A request to the Conservation Department resulted in an investigation. The investigation revealed that the three young sons of the farmer, growing up, turned their surplus energies to trapping as a way of picking up spare cash. The big catch they were making were skunks, and as a result of their efforts the boys kept the skunks pretty well cleared out. Skunks love eggs, and they had been doing a good job of cleaning out the nests of snapping-turtles around the pond. With the disappearance of the skunks, the snapping-turtles thrived and multiplied, with the result that the pond became a danger-spot to be avoided by migratory ducks.

This story is an interesting example of what happens in nature when her delicate balance is disturbed, and is pertinent because the common house cat is only too often a disturber of nature's balance. In nature, insects are normally controlled by birds, for insects form a large part of the normal diet of most birds. Cats, kept and protected by man, prey on the birds, and as a result the bug population flourishes. The harm the cat does is really two-fold; for while the birds killed (and a good cat can be expected to kill better than fifty birds a year, according to the Massachusetts Audubon Society) are of prime importance, the effect the cats have of keeping birds away from the premises bears even greater weight in the matter of the bug population.

In my experience, if rats and mice constitute a problem on the premises, an intelligent program of trapping and poison will prove more effective in controlling them than will cats. In any event, I am certain that there is no justification for keeping a house cat around the place if you have a garden. There are plenty of sentimental justifications perhaps, but sentiment will not grow vegetables.

Experience shows with sad certainty that natural control of insects is not adequate for the gardener; he has to get out and kill bugs on his own account or he will have no garden. There are two ways to do this. One is by the use of insecticides, and the other is by hand-picking. In the preceding chapter the enemies of each vegetable were discussed, together with their control; but an understanding of the general aspects of the problem will enable the gardener to modify guide-book suggestions to his own uses.

Hand-picking plays a relatively small part of pest control ordinarily, but in the small garden it can be very effective. Certain large beetles and worms, conspicuous egg-clusters, and some moths and butterflies, can be combated directly, by hand-to-hand combat as it were. For instance, the familiar white cabbage-worm butterfly, which is always seen pirouetting its dance of destruction over the cabbage in the early summer, can be combated by hand. A tennis racquet makes an extremely effective weapon. Each dead butterfly is the equivalent of a hundred or more dead cabbage worms. Inspection of the crucifers for eggs, which are yellow clusters laid on the under-side of the leaves, is the next step. Finally, after the worms are hatched, a great number of them can be destroyed by hand-picking, without a great deal of time or trouble being expended.

The Colorado potato beetle, which sometimes attacks the to-mato plant, can be controlled by hand-picking on tomatoes. The large green hornworm, or tomato worm, who wears a horn on his back, can also be controlled by hand-picking.

For the most part, however, the control of insects will be by the use of insecticides, which are applied either in the form of dust or as liquid spray. These insecticides are in general of two main types—stomach poisons and contact poisons. Stomach poisons are effective against insects which eat the leaves; con-tact poison against those that suck the juice of the plant.

Of the two methods of application, I prefer the dust method, although there are drawbacks to either system. Liquids are messy to handle and are heavy; and ordinarily an adequate sprayer is more expensive than a duster and considerably more trouble to maintain in working condition. Dust, on the other hand, cannot be applied during windy weather, and is best applied when the leaves are moist with dew. There are several types of inexpensive dusters which are adequate for use in the small garden; the type which has a quart glass jar as a re-ceptacle for the dust is the kind I have used with complete satisfaction.

I have never attempted home-mixing of insecticides or fungi-cides. The amount of materials used in the garden does not, in my opinion, warrant the trouble and study required. As a matter of fact, any first-rate manufacturer of spray or dusting materials will offer a complete line of dusts and sprays which will adequately take care of all the requirements of the or-dinary garden.

Beginners are sometimes confused, in ordering an insecticide, as to whether their need is for the control of an "aphid" or an "aphis." The aphis and the aphid are so closely related that they are almost one and the same, and poison for one will control the other. The variety which plagues the vegetable garden is commonly known as the leaf-hopper. I mention this, for in ordering commercial sprays and dusts, it is necessary for you to know what the different pests listed in the control charts are. One chart will list the aphis, another the aphid, while you are thinking of the leaf-hopper, all of which makes for confusion.

Keep in mind these keys to good insect control:

1. *Inspect plants regularly* to keep abreast of pest buildup. Control aphids and mites before they become numerous.

2. *Select the proper insecticide.* Know the pest (s) to be controlled and choose recommended pesticides.

3. *Apply insecticides when good weather exists.* Spray when wind is less than 5 miles per hour. Dust only when wind is calm. Do not treat plants during the hottest part of the day or when they are wilted. Rain washes insecticides from plants, which means that retreatment may be necessary.

4. *Cover plants with insecticide.* Apply treatment to all plant surfaces because many pests feed only on the underside of leaves.

5. *Treat only when necessary* to prevent or control insect injury. Apply only the recommended dosage. More will not improve control but is dangerous to handle, may burn plants, and may leave harmful residues on fruits at harvest.

6. Although useful, all insecticides are poisons and must be treated as such. *Always read the container label before applying any insecticide.*

Insecticides are chemicals that poison insects or spider mites when applied according to label directions. Some are more specific than others for the control of certain pests and knowledge of this makes control more effective. For example: Sevin is effective for worm (caterpillar) control; Diazinon, malathion, or Thiodan are all effective for aphid control; and Kelthane is best for spider mite control.

Most insecticides are available as emulsifiable concentrates, wettable powders, and dusts that can be purchased at garden supply stores.

Sprays are purchased as emulsifiable concentrates (liquid) or wettable powders (dry) and a small quantity of either is mixed with water at home just before applying. Shake emulsifiable concentrate container before using. Emulsifiable concentrates form a milky-white emulsion when mixed with water that requires little if any further stirring.

Wettable powders should be mixed thoroughly with a small amount of water until a paste is formed that is then mixed with water in the spray tank. Wettable powders tend to settle out in water, therefore, shake the spray tank frequently during the application. Some wettable powders contain a mixture of insecticide plus fungicide. Such combinations are called *all-purpose mixtures* and are useful when more than one pest requires control at one time.

Mix only what is needed for the immediate spray job because many insecticides lose their effectiveness if left in water overnight.

Dusts are dry formulations of insecticides that require no mixing with water. They are applied to plants as purchased. Apply dusts with a rotary crank, bellows, or plunger-type duster.

It is best to apply dust during the early morning or evening when plants are damp with dew and when wind is calm.

Always store insecticides in their original containers and keep bags and bottles tightly closed. In summer store them in a cool, dry place *away from the reach of children and pets*. In winter, store liquid insecticides in a reasonably warm place, preferably away from the house.

Wrap empty insecticide containers in newspaper and place in trash cans that are emptied by a refuse collection service. Do *not* burn empty pesticide containers.

Several types of sprayers are useful in the home vegetable garden. Decide your needs before purchasing one. *Continuous sprayers* or hand atomizers (flit-gun type) are satisfactory for small gardens. They are designed for spraying emulsifiable concentrates but not wettable powders since they tend to clog the nozzle. Choose a sprayer made of noncorrosive material that is easily cleaned. *Compressed air sprayers* are useful for large gardens. The spray made from emulsifiable concentrate or wettable powder is expelled by air pressure supplied by a built-in hand pump. The reservoir tanks vary in size to hold from one to five gallons of spray. Choose a sprayer that is easily cleaned and one for which replacement parts can be purchased in succeeding years.

To prolong the life of the sprayer, drain excess spray after using in an area away from children, pets, and wildlife. Flush the tank with water several times and force water through the spray wand and nozzle until the water is clear. Finally, to avoid rust or corrosion, suspend the tank upside down with the lid removed to permit drainage and drying. *Hose-on applicators* are jars or bottles that connect to garden hoses. They are satisfactory when applying emulsifiable concentrates but are less effective for applying wettable powders.

If the gardener has tended his garden well, has cultivated it and battled the pests, if no major upset of nature, such as extreme drought, frost or flood has interfered, he is now ready to enjoy the fruits of the garden. In fact, this enjoyment is a continuous process: the first vegetables are ready for the table while the cultivation of other varieties is proceeding. Gradually, however, his labors lessen, until the time comes when the task of cultivation is finished and the growing of the vegetables can be considered complete.

CHAPTER V

USING GARDEN PRODUCTS

IT MIGHT seem that no one needs to be told about using garden products. We are all using them every day. The only difference might appear to be that we either buy them at the grocery-store or raise them in our own flourishing garden.

That is not all there is to it, however; for if you buy vegetables, you buy only for your immediate needs and only at the time the need arises. Garden produce, on the other hand, is lavishly supplied by nature in quantities greater than can possibly be used at once, and you have a satisfying surplus on hand.

Within the limitations of the season and the crop, the time that the garden products are ready for use can be modified by the selection of varieties and by successive plantings. But there will always be a surplus if the garden is well cared for. The use of this surplus is of great importance for two reasons. The first and more obvious is because waste is foolish; the second is because by the proper handling of surpluses the usefulness of the garden can be greatly extended. Should we only use the fruits of the garden as they mature, we would gain direct benefits from it for only two or three months. Proper handling of the surplus, on the other hand, extends the use of the garden produce through all twelve months of the year.

In some cases surplus vegetables can be sold; but that comes under market gardening and we are concerned here only with the subsistence garden.

The first step in the using of a crop of any kind is, of course, its harvesting. While the harvesting of a small garden presents no great problem, there are a few things to bear in mind. In the first place, practically all vegetables are better when they are young than when fully matured. They are more tender and juicy and more delicious in flavor. One gardener I knew was so delighted with the lovely plants he raised that he could not bear to use them. Nothing was ever picked until it was as big as it would grow, and consequently past its prime as something to eat. It is all right to grow large turnips, for instance, and plenty of them—provided you do not forget that their primary destiny is to be eaten.

The first vegetables you will enjoy from the garden are the "thinnings." Lettuce thinnings will be the earliest, followed by spinach thinnings, then beet thinnings used as greens. Radishes will appear with the early thinnings, but they present no problem of either storage or harvesting. Carrots need not be thinned until the largest roots are lead-pencil size at the top; the larger roots can then be served raw. They are delicious.

This first carrot thinning need not be final; a subsequent thinning a week or two weeks later will yield another crop of pencilings for salad use, and a fair number of roots the size of a finger. These carrots can be canned whole. Carrots properly canned at this stage of their growth will afford the family a real treat in the winter. This is true also of beets. The second thinning, when the roots are the size of marbles up to walnuts, will provide a delectable dish for the table, and if there is a surplus these baby beets are delicious canned.

Onions can be used from the time they are large enough to eat as scallions until they are stored for winter. The first thinnings are tiny scallions; the second and principal thinning should produce scallions the size of a lead-pencil and larger. Two fifty-foot rows will yield more than the average family can use. From this point on through the season until the onions are gathered, they can be served as a cooked vegetable, and will also provide small onions for pickling.

Spinach will be ready for use along with the other early vegetables and can be used as thinned. Early in the season the first peas will be ready. Young tender peas are the best, but they should not be picked before the pods are well filled. Before the last of the early peas are quite gone, the first of the late peas should be ready for picking. As soon as the early peas are finished, as explained before, the vines should be pulled and placed on the compost pile if they are not diseased. The brush can be pulled and burned. The space thus made available can then be used for setting out late cabbage plants and for a second planting of beets, carrots, lettuce, or radishes, as is desired.

Summer squash produce early (cocozelle squash can be picked when eight inches long) and continue well through the summer till frost comes. The fruit should never be allowed to grow too large; it should be picked while the outside skin is still tender. There will be a surplus above the immediate requirements, and this should be canned; cocozelle squash is one of the prime canned vegetables.

Small cucumbers suitable for pickling, and soon afterward larger ones for table use, will be available.

Waxbeans will be the first of the beans to be ready. Snapbeans are best when they are tiny; therefore as soon as they have grown three or four inches long they are ready for use. They grow very rapidly and are prolific, so it will be necessary to can the surplus at the time when the beans are still young and tender. Waxbeans may also be permitted to mature and dry on the vines to be used as shell beans. In picking beans it is well to remember that the leaves should not be touched while they are wet.

The pole snapbeans will come next, and with them will be the early corn. Sweet corn is ready to pick ordinarily when the silk is black and dried all the way down to the husk. This is not, I have found, an infallible test, and the selecting of properly ripened ears is sometimes quite a problem to the novice. The safest way is to grasp the ear around its middle. If the ear feels solid and well filled-out, it is probably ready for the pot. Corn should never be gathered more than two hours before cooking; an hour or a half-hour is even better.

A few simple calculations prove that sweet corn produces less in terms of space and labor than anything else growing in the garden. And in addition it probably takes more out of the soil than any other vegetable. It requires a dozen or more ears of corn to produce enough cut corn to fill a quart jar. It takes roughly three hills of corn to produce twelve ears, and it takes about sixteen square feet of garden to support three hills of corn. Thus it is apparent that the return in terms of pleasure and enjoyment must be very high to warrant the time and space devoted to the growing of corn.

I do not believe that old Dr. Johnson would agree that it is wise to devote one-quarter of a restricted garden space to the growing of sweet corn. But the majority of Americans, loving their corn on the cob as they do, would disagree with Dr. Johnson. In spite of the amount of space devoted to the growing of corn on our garden plan, it is doubtful if there will be much of a surplus to can for winter use.

Shell beans should be allowed to mature and dry on the plant. The plants should then be pulled and piled in loose windrows to dry before being put under cover. Another system is to set a stake, four or five feet long, in the ground in the bean patch, the top end sharpened as well as the earth end. The beans are then pulled and each handful of dried plants speared down over the stake, but not permitted to touch the ground. The process is similar to spearing a paper on the old-fashioned bill-file. After the pods have thoroughly dried they may be shelled on the spot, or removed to the shed or cellar where they may be shelled at leisure.

Shell beans are sometimes used green; the horticultural bean in particular is good green, and is somewhat similar to the limabean in taste. Shell beans are also good canned. If the surplus crop is to be canned, they should be picked when mature but before they are dried.

Of the limabeans the bush limas will be ready for the table first. By the time the last of the bush limas are gone the pole limas will come along. These beans, while they are delicious, do not produce bountifully in terms of food on the table; for while it is easy to pick a bushel of pods, the bushel shells out in disproportionately and disappointingly few beans.

Summer cabbage may be used as soon as the heads are firm and solid. The plant should be pulled, the stem and the outside leaves being consigned to the compost pile.

Cauliflowers are harvested as soon as the heads are of sufficient size to be used. Like cabbage, the stalk and outside leaves should go on the compost pile. Surpluses of cauliflower may be canned very successfully; and some portion of the crop may be preserved for winter use by using it in mixed pickles.

Parsnips and salsify will mature in time to be used on the table; they can be pulled and stored for winter use as well, but at least one-third of each row should be left in the ground for use early in the spring. Each of these vegetables improves in flavor by being frozen in the ground.

Turnips will probably find little use on the table during the season, for there are too many other, more desirable vege- tables available at the same time. They will keep in storage better than most vegetables, however, and their main value is therefore for winter use.

Tomatoes, as included in this garden, are grown primarily for table use. They can be picked green, as has been mentioned, and ripened indoors; but they cannot successfully be stored for any length of time. The canning of tomatoes can be done so successfully and cheaply by commercial growers and canners that it does not ordinarily pay to can home-grown tomatoes. It seems that in the average garden a surplus of tomatoes is almost inevitable if the crop has done well. A small amount can be conserved as green-tomato pickle; beyond that, the surplus must either be canned or given away.

Parsley will be late in coming along, ordinarily, and can be used from the garden toward the end of the summer. In the late fall the leaves may be cut and dried and stored in tight jars. Or the plants may be transplanted into pots or boxes and grown indoors. In mild climates parsley can be left out all winter.

The use of a cold frame for extending the garden season has already been mentioned. A cold frame not only will bring the first green things to the table in the spring before they could be grown in the garden, but it also permits the use of trans- planted garden stuff long after the garden itself is bare and frozen. It is also useful for starting plants, such as early cabbage, broccoli, cauliflower, etc. Since a cold frame can be used for starting, for growing, and for storing vegetables, it forms a very valuable adjunct to the garden.

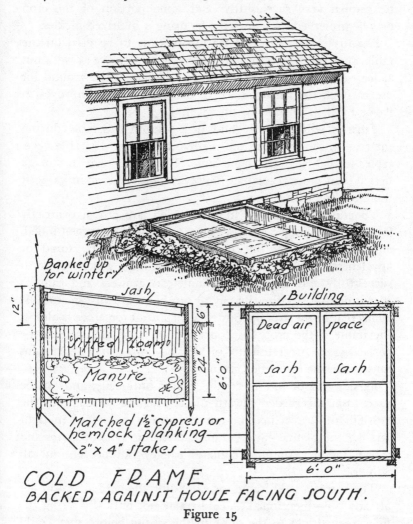

Banked up for winter

12″

sash

Sifted Loam

Manure

6″

24″

6′0″

Matched 1½″ cypress or hemlock planking

2″ x 4″ stakes

Building

Dead air space

Sash   Sash

6′0″

COLD FRAME
BACKED AGAINST HOUSE FACING SOUTH.

Figure 15

A cold frame is, in effect, a large shallow box with a glass top and no bottom. Stock hotbed sashes come three by six feet, and therefore the dimensions of the cold frame should be six feet in one direction and any desired multiple of three feet in the other direction. It is suggested that a frame suitable for a garden of the size under discussion would be a two-sash or three-sash frame. In other words, the dimensions would be six by six, or six by nine, depending upon whether two or three sashes were used.

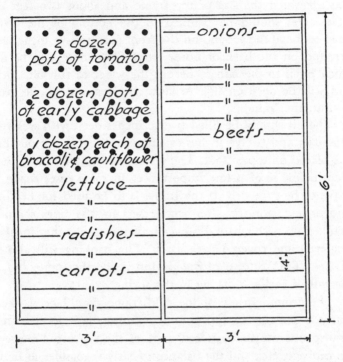

PLANTING PLAN FOR COLDFRAME

Figure 16

The cold frame can be a portable affair, but it is better if it is permanently located. The site chosen should be where it is protected from the prevailing winds on the north and west, and where it gets the spring sun. A wall of the house or shed may well form one side of the frame, if the right exposure can be had, and if there is good drainage, and protection from any eave drip. My cold frame is six by twelve, and the south wall of the woodshed forms one of its sides. The other three sides are of one and a half inch plank, eight inches wide. Scantlings, two by four inches, form the corners and the sash supports.

If a permanent cold frame is to be made, it is best that a pit be excavated the size of the frame and about two feet deep. The sides should be planked to the bottom of the pit; six inches above the ground on the front side, twelve inches above ground on the back or house side. Thus there will be a six-inch pitch to the sash to permit the water to run off, and the pit will be deep enough to keep the frost out of the ground within the frame.

The pit should be filled twelve inches deep with well-rotted manure; and twelve inches of sifted and fertile topsoil should be placed on top of that. The sash must be easily movable, for ventilation is of prime importance. In some cases shade may have to be provided. If the frame is to be used for heeling-in greens, etc., for use after winter sets in, the sides should be banked up with cornstalks over leaves or some other insulating material and covered with earth. The banking will also help to keep the frost out of the ground inside the frame and thus permit of earlier working in the spring.

The ground inside of the cold frame should be worked as early as possible in spring and put into shape for seeding. If transplants are to be raised, part of the space can be seeded to cabbage, etc., and the balance to early vegetables to be used directly from the frame, as though it were a little garden. A suggested plan for planting a six-by-six-foot cold frame is shown in the diagram.

A half-inch board, four inches wide and three feet long, with a small block nailed to the center of it to be used as a handle is extremely useful in planting the cold frame. The board is used for a guide in making furrows. It is laid on the earth, and a pointed stick is run along its edge, resulting in a straight furrow for the planting of the seeds. The board is then moved and another furrow is made, the width of the board from the first one. Thus the rows come out straight and evenly spaced four inches apart.

After the early lettuce, radishes, beets and carrots have been used and the sets have been transplanted, the soil of the cold frame should be kept free from weeds throughout the summer. In the fall, after the first frost and before the hard freeze, the lettuce, chicory or endive, parsley, onions, Swiss chard, etc., may be heeled-in close together, the sash closed, and the frame banked up. Thus the use of fresh garden salads and greens may be extended well into the winter.

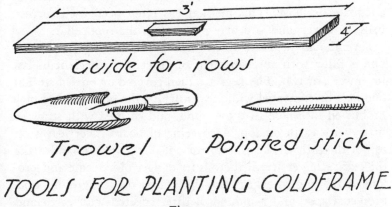

Guide for rows

Trowel   Pointed stick

TOOLS FOR PLANTING COLDFRAME

Figure 17

Thus far five general methods of the use of vegetables have been discussed. The first and most important is that direct from the garden to the table, and includes the early use of the cold frame. The second and third methods are canning and pickling. The fourth is that of transplanting to the cold frame after the outdoor season is over. The fifth method, that of storage, is properly divided into two sections, dry storage and moist storage.

Dry storage presents no problem to the average householder. All types of dried beans, dried parsley and onions are stored in this way. Onions, after they have been harvested and dried, should be kept in some dry frost-proof place. This may be the pantry or the attic. Shell beans, when thoroughly dry, can be placed in tins if there is danger from mice and rats, and stored in the same place. Dried parsley in jars can be kept with the canned vegetables.

Moist storage, on the other hand, may present some difficulties to the average householder. Vegetables on the plan which require moist storage are parsnips, salsify, beets, carrots, turnips and cabbage. Moist cool storage can be provided by several different methods out of doors, or by a properly constructed root-cellar in the house. I have tried the outdoor system only once, and the attempt was unsuccessful, partly because of the extreme cold of this climate and partly because of the lack of adequate drainage. This method has often been used successfully, however, and you may prefer it to the root-cellar.

Several nail kegs are lined with paper or straw, and each one is filled with an assortment of vegetables sufficient to last for a week or two. The kegs are then covered or buried so that one may be excavated without disturbing the others. They may be buried in a hole in the ground, and covered with straw or litter, with earth on top. A covering of boards over leaves on top of the soil will keep the frost out of the ground and make the excavating easier. If there is no danger of extreme and prolonged freezing, the kegs may be placed on the ground in a protected spot, and a mound of litter covered with earth and boards heaped over them.

The chief things to be remembered are that the temperature should be between thirty-two degrees and forty degrees, and that the air should be moist. Any plan or system which can produce these conditions will be adequate.

More often used for vegetable storage is a cold room in the cellar. Again varying problems are presented, depending principally upon the climate but also upon other factors. Reduced to the simplest elements, a corner of the cellar may be partitioned off so that the heat of the furnace does not raise the temperature there, for a temperature of not over forty degrees must be maintained. Two other factors are moisture and ventilation. The best arrangement is to have an earth floor in the cold room; in this way the proper moisture content of the air is automatically maintained.

There can be no hard-and-fast rule given for arrangements to be made in setting up the cold room. For instance, in my cold cellar, there is no trouble in keeping the temperature down; in fact, I have had freezes. A common country practice in this climate is to store roots in barrels of sand placed in the

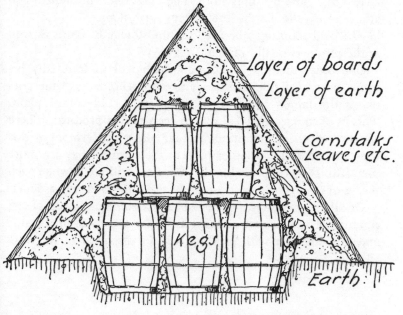

CROSS SECTION OF OUTDOOR VEGETABLE STORAGE IN NAIL KEGS

Figure 18

cold room. Cabbages may be hung from the ceiling of the cold room by their roots, having been pulled and not trimmed of their outside leaves. If barrels of sand are used for the roots, danger of fungus rot is lessened if the sand is changed each year.

The construction of a cold room adequate for the storage of roots and cabbage is simple and inexpensive. If your cellar has a bay under a bay-window, simply build a double partition of wallboard across the bay, leaving a door for easy access. If there is no bay, a corner six by six can be partitioned off in the same manner, with a door in one of the two walls. If the cellar floor is cement, the proper amount of moisture can be maintained by the frequent sprinkling of water on the floor; or the floor can be covered with a layer of peat moss, which can be purchased at a garden supply store. The moss, once moistened, will afford an excellent substitute for an earth floor.

The cold room may be used for the storage of fruits as well as the products of the garden.

One other method of storing, which will undoubtedly become more available to the average householder as time goes on, is the family locker in a community cold-storage plant. This is, of course, the ideal way to keep garden products. There are three of these community storage plants in Vermont at this time and no doubt in other parts of the country they are more plentiful. It seems probable that the time will come when such means of storage will be reasonably available to every gardener.

Of all the methods mentioned for extending the use of the produce of the garden, canning is by far the most important; and this, together with pickling, will be discussed in the next chapter.

CHAPTER VI

COOKING, CANNING AND PICKLING

THIS IS NOT a cook book. There is, nevertheless, a definite relationship between the garden and the dining-room table; and the kitchen stove plays a major part in that relationship. From the gardener's point of view, no small part of the stove's importance is its use in pickling and canning, for it is by these means of conserving vegetables that the fullest use of the garden is achieved. Preparing food for the table is of less interest to him.

Ordinarily, however, the householder buying vegetables is not confronted with the same kind of problem as is the householder who has the produce of the garden to work with; so it seems advisable to give a few brief suggestions on the cooking of some of the vegetables listed on the plan.

Limabeans, peas, corn on the cob—these need no champion, and probably there will never be a surplus of them. But they form actually only a small part of the produce of the garden, and are in fact among the least rewarding of all in terms of labor and food value. A distinction should be made between subsistence gardening and luxury gardening.

The average American home-cooking does not do well by vegetables. This is largely a question of point of view, vegetables being regarded more as a source of nourishment and vitamins than as a real gastronomical treat in their own right. It is true that the best effects are gained by the liberal use of milk, cream and butter; but there is a balance to be struck, and in many instances a rather lavish treatment of vegetables will result in such tasty dishes that the net effect is economic gain, for expensive meats can be left off the menu. This is particularly true if the vegetables are home-grown and home-canned. Vegetables can be so prepared that a meal without meat will be exciting as well as nourishing.

PARSNIPS

Parsnips are a highly underrated vegetable, at least in this country. The reason must lie in the way they are prepared for the table, for at our house many people have enjoyed parsnips who had always disliked them before. To be at their best, parsnips should be frozen in the ground. They are perfectly good late in the fall, but the flavor is improved by freezing.

The favorite way of serving parsnips in this house is to make them into a stew, similar to an oyster stew, with butter, milk and cream.

Parsnip Stew

Dice two cups of parsnips, add a small onion and a clove of garlic finely chopped, and cook until tender. Add a cup of cream, salt and pepper, two tablespoonfuls of butter, and two cups of milk; bring the whole to a boil, and then you have a very fine dish indeed.

Parsnips with Roast

Scrape the parsnips and cook them around an oven roast, along with the potatoes. Baste the parsnips and turn them in the juice of the roast occasionally.

Fried Parsnips

Scrape the parsnips and boil them rapidly until they are tender. Drain and reheat them in a frying-pan with brown butter, which has had a small clove of garlic cut fine and added to it.

SALSIFY

The little-known salsify, or vegetable oyster, is another vegetable which can be dug from the ground in the spring, for it improves with freezing. Salsify needs rich seasoning, but it warrants it.

Baked Salsify

Scrape and dice the salsify and boil until tender. Prepare a rich cream sauce, add the tender boiled salsify to the cream sauce. Place all in a baking-dish and cover the top with broken crackers, salt, pepper and plenty of butter. Brown in the oven.

ONIONS

Young onions can be used with great satisfaction as a cooked vegetable. For this purpose they should be pulled as soon as the bulb begins to form, say the size of a marble or a walnut. The onions should then be trimmed so that two or three inches of the stalk remains. These are the raw materials for a delicious dish of spring onions served in a novel way.

Spring Onions

Remove the outside skins and boil rapidly until the onions are tender. Serve with salt, pepper, and plenty of butter. These young onions are unbelievably sweet and delicate in flavor, and will not disturb the most frail digestion, as green onions are apt to do.

French Fried Onions

The same young spring onions may be used for French frying, again leaving at least two inches of stem with the bulb. These onions, fried in the usual way, will be found to have an entirely different and far better flavor than if mature onions are used.

LETTUCE

If the lettuce crop gets beyond the family requirements for salads, it may be served cooked, thus adding variety to the menu.

Brown Lettuce

Shred the lettuce fine and put it into a frying-pan with brown butter and a tiny bit of garlic. Or instead of butter use finely chopped bacon, together with the fat but not too much of the fat.

Or lettuce may be used as boiled greens:

Braised Lettuce

Fry in butter a small onion and a clove of garlic chopped very fine. Shred the lettuce, place it in a saucepan and bring to a rapid boil. Add the chopped onion. When tender drain, and serve with salt, pepper and butter. On account of its high moisture content lettuce cooks down to much less bulk than many other garden greens, and so more is required for the same number of servings.

SWISS CHARD

Swiss chard is in common enough use as boiled greens by those who grow it in their gardens. It is seldom found on the shelves of the green-grocer, however, and while it is similar to beet greens or spinach, it may be wise to include it in our list of recipes.

Swiss Chard Greens

Place the washed chard leaves in boiling water, turning the leaves from time to time. A little fried chopped bacon added with the salt and pepper as it is served enhances its flavor.

Swiss Chard Stems

If there is an abundance of chard and the family tires of eating it as greens, the leaves can be stripped from the tender stalks, which then can be cooked rapidly in boiling water over a hot fire, and served as is asparagus, with drawn butter, cream sauce, or hollandaise sauce.

SUMMER SQUASH

Cocozelle squash, which is little known and seldom if ever found on the market, is by far the most delicious and delicate of all the summer squash. If they are picked young, while the outside skin is still tender, and cooked at once, they require no fancy extras to give them choice flavor.

Boiled Squash

Wash the freshly picked squash, slice it thinly across, skin and all, and boil rapidly. Drain, chop, and serve with salt, pepper and butter.

Fried Squash

Brown a finely chopped onion in butter, add the thin slices of the squash to the frying-pan, and cook slowly under a cover, adding no water. Stir the squash occasionally and cook until tender.

CORN

Corn on the cob is probably the American national dish, but if the family should tire of this time-honored delicacy, there are several other delightful ways of serving corn—not even to mention that old New England favorite, succotash.

Creamed Corn

Cut the corn from the cob, add cream, salt and pepper, and bring to a boil over a slow fire.

Fried Corn

Brown a finely chopped small onion and a small piece of finely chopped garlic in butter, add the corn, and cook in a frying-pan over a very slow fire, stirring from time to time. Add salt and pepper.

Corn Pudding

Corn pudding is the best of them all, if it is properly made; but when it is properly made it is a luxury dish. The following recipe is rich but good.

Take two cups of cut corn, three tablespoonfuls of sugar, half a teaspoonful of salt, three eggs, and one cup of cream. Beat the yolks and whites of the eggs separately; add the cream, corn, sugar and salt to the beaten yolks. Fold in the beaten whites and cook in a hot oven as a soufflé.

Corn Chowder

To three cups of scalded milk add six slices of finely chopped crisp bacon, salt, pepper, a tablespoonful of flour, and two cups of corn. Simmer for about half an hour, and the result is a rich, filling soup.

CARROTS

Carrots are ordinarily considered an uninteresting dish. This is probably because in most cases they are cooked too long. A proper way to prepare carrots is to cut them into long thin strips, like shoestring potatoes, and boil them as rapidly as possible, until tender. Serve only with salt, pepper and butter, and you will have a rare treat.

The pencilings, or baby carrots the size of a lead-pencil, are delicious cooked. Take baby carrots, cook until tender, and serve with a cream sauce with a dash of vinegar added.

CABBAGE

The secret of tasty cabbage dishes is rapid cooking. For that reason cabbage should be finely shredded and cooked over a very hot fire. Be sure the water is boiling rapidly before the cabbage is dropped in.

Baked Cabbage

Boil the cabbage as indicated; drain and chop. Cover with a rich cream sauce; place the cabbage and cream in a baking-dish and cover with small pieces of bread, salt, pepper and butter, and brown in the oven. This is a noble dish.

Special Cabbage Salad

Shred a large head of cabbage; add a finely chopped small onion and a dash of garlic. Add French dressing, and serve as a relish with fish or meat. It is especially good with soft-shell crabs, and with fried meats of all kinds.

Cabbage Cups

For a novel *hors d'œuvre,* which will prove to be immensely popular, select a firm head of cabbage from the garden; peel off the outer leaves, and excavate a deep hollow in it at the stem end. Fill this cabbage shell or cup with mayonnaise dressing and place it on a dish, surrounded with small pieces of cauliflower, broken from a head fresh from the garden. These cauliflower sprigs should be scrubbed and soaked in cold salt water. The procedure then is to dip the cauliflower sprigs in the mayonnaise and eat them as long as they last. That will not be long!

SPINACH

Spinach, like peas, is so good when fresh from the garden that it needs no special treatment to make it delicious. It should be cooked quickly. The washed leaves should be added to rapidly boiling water, and there should not be more than two inches of water in the bottom of the saucepan. As the spinach wilts, it should be turned in the water.

Creamed Spinach

Take spinach, cooked as above, drain it and chop fine. Add a tiny bit of shredded garlic and some heavy cream. Let the spinach stand on the back of the stove in a double-boiler until the flavor of the cream has penetrated. Try adding a sprinkling of grated nutmeg, and see if you like this unusual flavor.

BEANS

Stringbeans, cut square and indifferently allowed to cook slowly, are the basis of the average person's idea of what snap-beans taste like. If the beans are cut in long, very thin strips, and cooked rapidly over a hot fire, they are an entirely different vegetable and an infinitely more delicious one.

Stringbeans are a common item on the family menu. Shell beans, on the other hand, with the exception of baked beans, are strangers to the average family. To discover their manifold possibilities, shell beans must be grown in your own garden. It is almost impossible to buy them except when they are dried, and those are usually served either baked or as bean soup. Shell beans, however, matured on the vine but not permitted to dry, afford one of the most substantial and at the same time delicious dishes that the garden has to offer.

Creamed Shell Beans

Shell the beans out of the pods as peas are shelled. Boil until tender; add cream, salt and pepper, and then cook over a slow fire until the flavor of the cream saturates the beans. Milk and butter may be substituted for the cream.

Kidney beans, horticultural beans, or ripe stringbeans may be used with uniformly good results.

TOMATOES

The unripe fruit of the tomato can be used if frost threatens; and if the following recipe is once tried, I feel certain that green tomatoes will be picked and used even when there is no danger of losing the crop by frost.

Fried Green Tomatoes

Slice, and dip each side of the slices in flour; sprinkle with salt and pepper, and fry in very hot fat until crisp. Drain on paper, then place on a platter and cover with cream sauce.

Or slice, and dip each side of the slices in cornmeal; sprinkle with salt and pepper and a little sugar; fry as above; drain on paper, and serve with a strip of crisply fried bacon.

With the hope that these few recipes and ways of preparing vegetables for the table may increase the consumption of the fresh produce of the garden, we will consider the next important step, for it is by the canning of surplus vegetables that the fullest use of the garden is enjoyed.

For home canning a pressure cooker is a necessity. By its use a great saving of both fuel and time is effected. Canning with an adequately large pressure cooker is no longer the hot and tedious chore that it was to the housewife of the past generation. The importance of having an adequately large cooker cannot be overemphasized. A family of five, using a garden of the size indicated, should require an eight-quart pressure cooker. The price of the cooker is soon saved in fuel and saved all over again in time.

The first vegetable to demand the attention of the canner

will be spinach. At about the same time that the spinach will be ready for the table, beet greens and Swiss chard will also be producing greens for table use, so it is certain that the first planting of spinach will provide a surplus for canning. It will take approximately a bushel of spinach or other greens to fill five quart jars.

It is difficult to make any estimate as to quantities involved, for there are variable factors—the yield, and the amount used fresh. Two fifty-foot rows of first-rate spinach should produce from six to eight bushels. The thinnings of two fifty-foot rows of beets should produce about one more bushel of greens. The Swiss chard is a continuous producer and during the season will probably yield eight to ten bushels. Thus the total estimated amount of greens available for use from the first planting of the garden should be fifteen to eighteen bushels. Of this amount probably ten bushels will be available for canning.

Canning ten bushels of greens sounds like an arduous undertaking; but it need not all be done at once. There can be two or three sessions of canning, and the total amount of greens for family use from the first planting should be about fifty quarts. There will be a second planting of both spinach and beets, which can be relied upon for an additional ten or fifteen quarts.

There will be a slight surplus of early beets and carrots available for canning. These vegetables should be canned while still young and tender, and at least eight or ten quarts of each should be conserved in this way for use as a winter delicacy.

The next vegetable requiring attention after the greens are under control will be the stringbeans. The wax beans first, and then the pole beans. Here again it is impossible to predict exactly what may be expected, for there are several ways in which the beans may be used and canned. Stringbeans may be canned green or allowed to mature and be canned as shell beans. Then, too, the amount of the crop and the immediate use must be known before any estimate of canning can be made.

However, it is certain that if the wax beans produce a normal crop there will be a surplus for canning green; and soon after they have come to the height of their productivity, the *Kentucky Wonder* will begin to produce. The *Kentucky Wonder* is very prolific, and when the vines are in full bearing there will be another canning crisis; for, to be good, stringbeans must be canned when young and tender. If they outdistance the canner they can be left on the vines to mature and be harvested then for canning as shell beans. Stringbeans, on the whole, including both the wax beans and the *Kentucky Wonder*, should produce a surplus sufficient for four dozen quarts; and this will not be too much.

The next vegetable to make demands upon the canner will be corn, and there should be a surplus to warrant the canning of two dozen quarts. The summer squash will have produced its first fruit long before this, but inasmuch as squash is a continuous producer there is no great rush of canning as far as it is concerned. Squash can be used on the table as desired, and the surplus accumulated until there is sufficient on hand to warrant canning. The three hills should produce a surplus for the putting up of at least a dozen quarts.

Telephone peas will be ready for canning before the corn, but it is difficult to tell whether there will be any surplus. It requires about a bushel of peas to make five quarts, and two double fifty-foot rows will not produce too many bushels of peas at best. If the peas are prolific and yield a normal crop, there may be a surplus for canning, even sufficient to put up a dozen quarts. The early peas cannot be counted on for any surplus at all.

The last of all to require the labor of the canner will be the shell beans. As much of this crop as desired may be allowed to dry on the vine and then be shelled, but it is urged that at least part of the crop be canned. Also any snapbeans that were left on the vines should be canned and not dried. It would round out the store of canned vegetables nicely if there could be two dozen cans of shell beans. The balance of the bean crop may then be dried.

So much for a rough estimate of the amounts of canned vegetables to be had from the garden surplus. The process of canning itself—in the past a slow, cumbersome, uncertain and laborious undertaking—is now much easier and more certain. New standards in home-canning exist, and the result is that it is a simple matter for a family having a supply of vegetables available to enjoy a more abundant fare, with better balance and variety in their daily diet. The pressure cooker is the machine which has made this possible, and by its greatly superior efficiency it has definitely put the old-fashioned wash-boiler system out of business.

A family of five, as stated, should have an eight-quart pressure cooker. The estimates given total fifty quarts of various greens; ten quarts of young beets; ten quarts of young carrots; forty-eight quarts of various beans, shell and snap; twenty-four quarts of corn; twelve quarts of peas; and twelve quarts of squash. This makes a total of one hundred and sixty-six quarts for the winter use of the family. A good goal to aim at is two hundred quarts for a family of five, and experience may prove that the garden, if properly handled, will produce sufficient surplus to attain that goal.

Here are the approximate canning yields of the various vegetables listed:

Stringbeans, 1 bushel	16-20 quarts
Shell beans, 1 quart	1 quart
Spinach and other greens, 1 bushel	3- 5 quarts
Baby beets, 1 bushel	16-20 "
Baby carrots, 1 bushel	16-20 "
Corn (Golden Bantam), 1 dozen ears	1 quart
Peas (in pod), 1 bushel	5- 6 quarts
Squash, two	1 quart

It is not necessary here to go into detailed instructions for the canning of each vegetable. A manual for the use of the cooker comes with each machine sold, and explicit directions for canning each vegetable are included.

Some vegetables which may be satisfactorily canned are not always included in the manuals. Among these are celery, cauliflower and broccoli. Cauliflower and broccoli each should be processed for forty minutes at a pressure of ten pounds. Celery should be processed for one hour at a pressure of ten pounds.

Certain of the products of the garden can be conserved for winter use by pickling. The vegetables which are ordinarily pickled are cabbage, beets, cauliflower, cucumbers, green tomatoes, green onions, and stringbeans. There are quantities of different recipes available for all the different kinds of pickles. The garden will provide an adequate supply of any or all of these vegetables to take care of the family pickle needs.

Sauerkraut is a nourishing food, and it is an excellent way to care for the surplus of the cabbage crop. It will keep indefinitely in a cool place, but for safety's sake it is well to can some of it. A dozen cans of sauerkraut might well be added to the list of canned vegetables.

To make sauerkraut, use the heads of mature cabbage. Remove the coarse leaves and wash the heads. Slice the cabbage with a knife, or shred with a slaw-cutter. Weigh the cabbage and for every ten pounds, add one-half cup of salt. Mix well and pack firmly into a crock or keg. Cover with a clean cloth and put a weighted cover over the cloth. Keep in a moderately warm place until fermentation ceases; that is, until bubbles no longer appear in the brine. This will take from ten to twenty days. Remove the scum every few days. If the brine does not cover the kraut, add enough weak brine (two tablespoonfuls of salt to a quart of water) to bring the liquid over the weighted cover.

After the sauerkraut has finished working, it is ready to be stored in a cool place, where it will keep indefinitely; or it may be canned and the jars added to the ever-growing store of canned vegetables and pickles which represent the householder's reserve. It is a reserve which will afford great satisfaction and pleasure to the family and will greatly reduce the amount of the annual food budget.

APPENDIX

Kind of Vegetable	Min. % Germination Considered Acceptable	Av. Life in Years	No. of Seeds Per Oz.	Seed for 100 ft.	Seed Per Acre	Plant for Forcing
Asparagus Seed	80	3	1250	½ oz.	5 lbs.	
Asparagus Roots	—	—	—	70 roots	5800	
Beans—Bush Snap	85	3	60–75	½ lb.	60–80 lbs.	
Beans—Pole Snaps	85	3	50–75	4 oz.	15–20 lbs.	
Beans—Bush Lima	80	2	24	1 lb.	95–110 lbs.	
Beans—Pole Lima	80	2	24	½ lb.	40–50 lbs.	
Beans—Bush Shell	85	3	50–75	½ lb.	60–90 lbs.	
Beets	70	4	1500	1 oz.	10 lbs.	
Broccoli	80	4	10000	¼ oz.	2 oz.	2/1–3/15
Brussels Sprouts	75	4	7000	¼ oz.	3 oz.	
Cabbage	80	4	8000	¼ oz.	4 oz.	2/15–3/15
Cabbage—Chinese	80	4	8000	¼ oz.	4 oz.	
Carrot	70	3	27000	¼ oz.	2–4 lbs.	
Cauliflower	75	4	10000	¼ oz.	4 oz.	2/15–3/15
Celery	65	3	75000	⅛–¼ oz.	2–4 oz.	2/1–3/1
Chard, Swiss	70	4	1100	½ oz.	4–6 lbs.	
Corn, Sweet	85	3	125	2 oz.	10–12 lbs.	
Corn, Pop	85	3	200	2 oz.	8–10 lbs.	
Cucumber	80	5	1000	½ oz.	2–3 lbs.	
Dandelion	75	3	35000	½ oz.	5–6 lbs.	7/1
Eggplant	65	4	5000	¼ oz.	3–4 oz.	3/1–4/1
Endive	75	5	15000	½ oz.	4–5 lbs.	
Kale	75	4	7500	½ oz.	4–5 lbs.	
Kohlrabi	80	3	8000	½ oz.	4–5 lbs.	
Lettuce—Loose Leaf	80	5	16000	¼ oz.	1½–2½ lbs.	2/15
Lettuce—Head	80	5	16000	¼ oz.	1–2 lbs.	2/15
Muskmelon	80	5	1200	½ oz.	2–3 lbs.	4/1
Watermelon	80	5	200	½ oz.	2 lbs.	4/1
Onion Seed	75	2	12000	½ oz.	4–5 lbs.	1/15–2/15
Parsley	65	1	17500	½ oz.	3–4 lbs.	
Parsnip	65	1	5600	½ oz.	4–6 lbs.	
Pea	85	3	90	½ lb.	90–150 lbs.	
Pepper	65	2	4000	⅛ oz.	5 oz.	3/15
Pumpkin	80	4	100	½ oz.	4 lbs.	
Radish	85	4	3500	1 oz.	12 lbs.	
Rutabaga	85	4	10000	¼ oz.	2 lbs.	
Salsify	75	1	4500	1 oz.	7–8 lbs.	
Spinach	70	3	3000	1 oz.	8–12 lbs.	
Spinach—N. Zealand	70	3	350	2 oz.	15 lbs.	
Squash—Summer	80	4	300	½ oz.	3–4 lbs.	
Squash—Winter	80	4	125	1 oz.	4 lbs.	
Tomato	80	3	7500	⅛ oz.	2 oz.	3/1–3/15
Turnip	85	4	10000	½ oz.	2–4 lbs.	

FOR GENERAL HOME GARDEN—Use Eastern States 5-10-10 at 15 to 25 lbs. per

† Courtesy of *Eastern States Cooperator*, Springfield, Mass.

* For these crops on soils of high fertility use the 10-10-10 mixture.

The relative lime requirements of each crop are indicated. Actual lime needs will vary with different soil and climatic conditions. Excessive acidity or excessive alkalinity should be overcome for all crops to assure greatest returns from fertilizer.

Soil tests will give growers information about lime and fertilizer requirements of their soils. Tests should be obtained when there is doubt about what soil needs.

Growers should recognize the importance of organic matter; to hold moisture, improve the

FERTILIZER

Plants from 1 Oz. Seed	Weeks to Grow Before Field Transplanting	Field Planting Dates	Inches Between Rows	Inches Apart in Row	Depth to Plant Seed Inches	Days to Harvest	Relative Lime Needs	Rate Per Acre in Cwt.	Analysis
800	1 year	4/1 -5/15	20-24	4	1	—	High	6-8	8-16-16
—	—	4/1 -5/15	60	18	4-6	2 yrs.	High	10-12	8-16-16
—	—	5/1 -7/15	30-36	3-4	1	45-55	Medium	3-4	8-16-8
—	—	5/15-7/1	48	4-12	1½	65	Medium	3-4	8-16-8
—	—	5/15-6/15	36-40	4	1-1½	75	Medium	4-5	8-16-8
—	—	5/15-6/1	48	4-12	1-1½	85	Medium	4-5	8-16-8
—	—	5/15-6/1	30-36	3-4	1-1½	85-95	Medium	3-4	8-16-8
—	—	4/1 -8/1	12-18	1½-3	½	55-70	High	8-12	8-16-16
5000	6 to 7	4/1 -6/15	36	24	½	60-100	Medium	8-10	8-16-8
3000	6 to 7	5/15-6/15	36	24	½	90-120	Medium	8-10	8-16-8
3000	5 to 7	4/1 -6/15	24	14-18	½	70-120	Medium	6-10	8-16-8*
3000	4 to 5	7/1 -8/1	24	14-18	½	75-90	Medium	6-10	8-16-8
—	—	4/15-7/15	12-15	1-2	¼	65-90	Medium	8-10	8-16-16
3000	5 to 7	4/1 -7/1	36	20	½	75-120	Medium	8-10	8-16-8
9000	4 to 5	5/1 -5/15	24-48	4-6	⅛	110-140	High	9-11	8-16-16
—	—	5/1 -6/1	24	4-6	½	55	High	8-12	8-16-8
—	—	5/1 -6/20	30-36	6-8	1	70-100	Medium	3-5	8-21-8
—	—	5/1 -6/1	30-36	6-8	1	100-120	Medium	3-5	8-24-8
—	—	5/1 -6/15	60	12	1½	50-70	Medium	7-9	8-16-8
—	—	8/1 -9/1	18-24	6-10	¼	175-210	High	8-10	8-16-8*
2000	8 to 10	5/15-6/1	36-50	24-36	½	70-80	Low	7-9	8-16-8
—	—	3/15-6/1	20	12	½	90-100	Medium	8-10	8-16-8*
—	—	7/15-8/1	30	18	½	55-65	Medium	8-10	8-16-8
—	—	4/1 -8/15	20	5	½	60	Medium	8-10	8-16-16
4000	5 to 6	4/1 -7/25	12	8-10	¼	60	Medium	9-11	8-16-8
4000	5 to 6	4/1 -7/15	12-15	12-18	¼	70-80	Medium	9-11	8-24-8
800	5 to 6	5/15-6/15	60	12	1	85-95	Medium	7-9	8-16-8
150	5 to 6	5/15-6/1	96	24	1	80-110	Low	4-6	8-16-8
1000	9 to 12	4/1 -5/1	20	4	½	120-180	High	8-12	8-16-16
—	—	4/1 -8/15	12	4-6	¼	120	Medium	8-10	8-16-8*
—	—	4/15-5/1	15-18	4	½	Winter	Medium	8-10	8-16-16
—	—	3/15-5/1	30-40	2-3	1	60-75	Medium	3-5	8-16-8
2000	8 to 9	5/15-6/1	30	20	½	60-80	Medium	4-6	8-16-8
—	—	5/15-6/1	96	24-36	1	110-120	Medium	4-6	8-24-8
—	—	4/1 -9/1	12	½	½	24-30	High	8-12	8-16-16
—	—	6/15-7/10	18-24	6-8	½	80-85	Medium	4-6	8-16-8
—	—	4/15-5/1	24	3	½	Winter	Medium	4-6	8-16-16
—	—	3/1 -9/15	14-18	2-4	½	40-50	High	9-11	8-16-8*
—	—	5/1 -6/1	48	36	1	75	High	9-11	8-16-8
—	—	5/15-6/15	48	12	1	50-65	Medium	7-9	8-16-8
—	—	6/1 -6/10	96	24	1	90-110	Medium	4-6	8-24-8
3000	7 to 9	5/15-6/1	48	24-40	½	65-90	Medium	7-9	8-24-8
—	—	4/1 -8/1	12-18	4-6	½	40-60	Medium	4-6	8-16-16

1000 sq. ft. or Eastern States 8–16–16 at 10 to 15 lbs. per 1000 sq. ft.

physical condition of soil, and to keep plant food in forms available to crops. When manure is a partial source of plant food it should be applied on crops that have a long growing season. Crops with a short growing season need more readily available plant food—which can be supplied by Eastern States fertilizer.

Note: This chart does not agree in all details with statements made in the text. The author stands by his recommendations, and offers the above chart, compiled by the Eastern States Cooperator, as a further and supplementary guide.

S. R. O.

COOPERATIVE EXTENSION WORK IN AGRICULTURE AND HOME ECONOMICS—STATE OF VERMONT

COLLEGE OF AGRICULTURE, UNIVERSITY OF VERMONT, AND
U. S. DEPARTMENT OF AGRICULTURE, COOPERATING

EXTENSION SERVICE,

SOIL TEST REPORT

Mr. S. R. Ogden,
Londonderry, Vermont, R. F. D. # 1   (THIS COPY FOR FARMER)

Dear Sir: Following is a report of tests on your samples of soil, together with recommendations for treatment.

	Sample of Box No. (1)	Sample or Box No. (2)	Sample or Box No. (3)
pH-Reaction	6.3 Mo. A.	6.3 Mo. A.	6.7 S. Ac.
Calcium	very high	very high	extra high
Nitrate Nitrogen	very low	very low	very low
Available Phosphorus	medium	medium	medium
Available Potash	medium	medium high	high
Other Tests			
....			
Texture	gravelly sandy loam	gravelly sand	gravelly sandy loam
No. Acres Represented in Sample			
Crop To Be Grown 1938	garden	garden	garden
Crop Grown 1937	"	"	"
Crop Grown 1936	"	"	"
Crop Grown 1935	"	"	"
Treatment 1937		M	M
Treatment 1936	M–F	M–F	M–F
Treatment 1935	M	M	M
Drainage	fair	good	good
Subsoil	hardpan	gravel	hardpan
Slope	slight pitch	to northeast.	

REMARKS:

RECOMMENDATIONS

Sample (1) is moderately acid. In order to bring this soil up to neutral or a little above neutral, it would be necessary to apply at least one ton of ground limestone per acre after the ground is plowed. To increase the essential elements for plant growth, I would advise applying not less than ten tons of manure to the acre (and if it could be hen manure, this would be better) plus 400 to 600 pounds of a 20% superphosphate. If manure is not available, apply 500 pounds per acre of a chemical fertilizer with the analysis 7-6-6.

Sample (2) is moderately acid. Same lime and fertilizer recommendations as No. 1.

Sample (3) is slightly acid. Same lime and fertilizer recommendations as No. 1.

JAS. A. MCKEE, County Agent

Amounts of mineral fertilizer to be used per unit:

Superphosphate	25 lbs. per 100 square feet
Potash	3 lbs. per 100 square feet
Nitrates	2 lbs. per 100 square feet

TENDERNESS TABLE

Vegetables Tender to Frost	Frost-resistant Vegetables
Corn	Artichokes
Beans of all kinds	Beets
Squash	Broccoli
Melons of all kinds	Brussels-sprouts
Cucumbers	Cabbage
Peppers	Carrots
Eggplant	Cauliflower
Tomatoes	Celery
Peas will resist some	Swiss Chard
	Chicory
	Endive
	Kale
	Kohlrabi
	Lettuce
	Onions
	Parsley
	Parsnips
	Radishes
	Rutabaga
	Spinach
	Salsify
	Turnips
	Peas will resist some

ROW DISTANCES AND SUCCESSION CROPS

Crop	Variety	No. of Rows	Succession Crop	Dist. bet. Rows
Lettuce	Black Seeded Simpson	½	Lettuce	12 inches
Radishes	Early Scarlet Globe	marker	None	12 inches
Parsnips	Improved Hollow Crown	1	None	12 inches
Radish	Early Scarlet Globe	½	Radish	12 inches
Salsify	Mammoth Sandwich Island	1	None	12 inches
Parsley	Paramount	½	None	12 inches
Onion	Early Grano	2	None	12 inches
Onion	Ebenezer	1	None	12 inches
Swiss Chard	Swiss Savoyed	1	None	12 inches
Summer Squash	Long Cocozelle	½	None	30 inches
Cucumber	Straight Eight	½	None	30 inches
Sweet Corn	Golden Bantam	5	None	24 inches
Sweet Corn	Stowell's Evergreen	5	None	24 inches
Beets	Crosby Early Wonder	1	Endive	12 inches
Beets	Detroit	1	None	12 inches
Carrots	Chantenay	1	Swiss Chard	12 inches
Carrots	Imperator	2	None	12 inches
Cabbage, early	Golden Acre (sets)	1	Head Lettuce	30 inches
Cabbage, late	Penn State Ballhead (sets)	—	None	30 inches
Cauliflower	Super Snowball (sets)	½	None	30 inches
Broccoli	Calabrese (sets)	½	None	30 inches
Beans, Lima	Fordhook (bush)	1	None	30 inches
Beans, Lima	King of Garden (pole)	1	None	36 inches
Beans, Snap	Kentucky Wonder (pole)	2	None	36 inches
Beans, Snap	Brittle Wax (bush)	1	None	24 inches
Beans, Shell	Geneva Red Kidney	1	None	24 inches
Beans, Shell	French's Horticultural	1	None	24 inches
Spinach	Dark Green Bloomsdale	2	Spinach	bet. rows
Spinach	Summer Savoy (second crop)	—	None	12 inches
Rutabaga	Macomber	½	None	12 inches
Peas	Alderman (tall)	2 double	Spinach	60 inches
Peas	World's Record (early)	1 double	Carrots and Beets	36 inches
Tomatoes		1	None	30 inches
			Late Cabbage	
Lettuce, second planting	Imperial 44	—	None	12 inches

DAYS TO HARVEST AND DEPTH TO PLANT

Crop	Variety	Days to Harvest	Depth
...tuce	Black Seeded Simpson	65	¼ inch
...dish	Early Scarlet Globe	24	½ inch
...snip	Improved Hollow Crown	150	½ inch
...ify	Mammoth Sandwich Island	270	½ inch
...sley	Paramount	120	¼ inch
...ion	Early Grano	120	½ inch
...ion	Ebenezer	125	½ inch
...ss Chard	Swiss Savoyed	55	½ inch
...mmer Squash	Long Cocozelle	65	1 inch
...cumber	Straight Eight	60	1½ inches
...et Corn	Golden Bantam	90	1 inch
...et Corn	Stowell's Evergreen	107	1 inch
...ts	Crosby Early Wonder	58	½ inch
...ts	Detroit	65	½ inch
...rots	Chantenay	68	¼ inch
...rots	Imperator	75	¼ inch
...ns, Lima	Fordhook (bush)	75	1½ inches
...ns, Lima	King of Garden (pole)	85	1½ inches
...ns, Snap	Kentucky Wonder (pole)	65	1½ inches
...ns, Snap	Brittle Wax (bush)	52	1 inch
...ns, Shell	Geneva Red Kidney	95	1–1½ inches
...ns, Shell	French's Horticultural	85	1–1½ inches
...ach	Dark Green Bloomsdale	38	½ inch
...ach	Summer Savoy	42	½ inch
...abaga	Macomber	80	½ inch
...s	Alderman	72	2–4 inches
...s	World's Record	60	2–4 inches

INDEX

Italicized numbers refer to the major
or most comprehensive treatments of entries.